Kimmy –

Happy 30th Birthday!!
As we both turn
30 this year I think
about people that never
made it to 30! We
can only be so greatful
that we have made it to
our 30th year. I've
read this book by
some inspiring women...
of there outlook and
wisdom of reaching
30. So I hope you
enjoy this read and
live to appreciate the
Big 3 0 ♡ Michele

# 30 Things

Every Woman Should
*Have* and Should *Know*
by the Time She's 30

# 30 Things

Every Woman Should
*Have* and Should *Know*
by the Time She's 30

*The Editors of* **GLAMOUR**
*and* PAMELA REDMOND SATRAN

**HYPERION**

NEW YORK

GLAMOUR is a registered trademark of Advance Magazine Publishers Inc. 30 THINGS EVERY WOMAN SHOULD HAVE AND SHOULD KNOW BY THE TIME SHE'S 30 is a trademark owned by Advance Magazine Publishers Inc.

Library of Congress Cataloging-in-Publication Data

Satran, Pamela Redmond.
    30 things every woman should have and should know by the time she's 30 / Pamela Redmond Satran and the editors of Glamour. — 1st ed.
        p. cm.
    ISBN 978-1-4013-2414-8
    1. Women—Psychology.   2. Experience.   3. Wisdom.   4. Life skills.   I. Glamour   II. Title.
    HQ1206.S275 2012
    646.70082—dc23

                                            2011047368

ISBN: 9781401324148

Hyperion books are available for special promotions and premiums. For details, contact the HarperCollins Special Markets Department in the New York office at 212-207-7528, fax 212-207-7222, or email spsales@harper collins.com.

FIRST EDITION

Book design by Judith Stagnitto Abbate / Abbate Design

Illustrations by Mary Lynn Blasutta

10   9   8   7   6   5   4   3   2

*For any woman turning thirty, remembering thirty,*
*or looking forward to thirty: We've got your back.*

# Contents

## By 30, you should have . . .

## What 30 means to me

**What 30 means to me**

**14** A skin-care regimen, an exercise routine, and a plan for dealing with those few other facets of life that don't get better after 30.

**15** A solid start on a satisfying career, a satisfying relationship, and all those other facets of life that *do* get better.

# By 30, you should know . . .

**1** How to fall in love without losing yourself.

**2** How you feel about having kids.

**3** How to quit a job, break up with a man, and confront a friend without ruining the friendship.

# Preface

BY CINDI LEIVE,
EDITOR-IN-CHIEF, *GLAMOUR*

Everyone loves lists. Our human history, in fact, has been shaped by them—from the Ten Commandments and the Ninety-Five Theses to the 282 tenets of Hammurabi's Code and the thirteen Articles of Confederation. Lists give shape to a sprawling, messy world; in modern life, there's the A-list, top-ten lists, blacklists, best-dressed lists, Craigslist, bucket lists, wish lists, and that albatross of daily existence, your to-do list.

But until 1997, there was no list specifically for women (unless you count the fifteen rules for serving your husband in *The Good Wife's Guide*, which I don't). That's when a *Glamour* columnist named Pam Satran sat down at her keyboard to write "30 Things Every Woman Should Have and Should Know by the Time She's 30." The List became a phenomenon, and while it may not have started a religious movement or founded a country, it actually *might* change your life, or at least the way you look at it.

I know it has changed mine. The month The List came out, I was a juniorish editor at *Glamour*, age, yes, thirty, and I remember reading the column while standing up in my office, holding the advance copy of the magazine and fully absorbed in Pam's catalog of essential items. (Something to wear if the employer of my dreams wanted to see me in an hour? Had that. But how *did* I feel about kids? And where *should* I go when my soul needed soothing?) Although I could not have predicted the reader response The List would generate, I knew it spoke to me—and I promptly xeroxed it for my oldest childhood friend, yet to turn thirty. I must not have remembered to send her the page, though, because a few months later, she sent The List to *me* in the form of a chain-mail forward, stripped of any attribution—but Pam's list word for word. "I love this!" my friend wrote. "I need a black lace bra."

As you'll hear, that email forward was just one stop on The List's ongoing viral journey around the globe. Over the past decade-plus, it's been wrongly attributed to everyone from Hillary Clinton to Maya Angelou. It's been taught in classrooms and stitched onto quilts. And most important, it's been read, and shared, by millions—because it distills the enormous, ever-changing question of how to be a happy, grown-up woman into essentials we can all check off, or at least consider.

I recently had the privilege of sitting in Carnegie Hall and watching the fabulous seventy-seven-year-old Gloria Steinem, an icon of the women's movement, receive a Lifetime Achievement honor at *Glamour*'s Women of the Year Awards. "In my generation, people thought that if you weren't married before you were thirty, you were a failure," she told the audience. "And now a lot of young women think that if they aren't seriously *successful* before thirty, they're a failure. So I want to say to you that there is life and dreams and surprises after thirty—and forty, and fifty, and sixty, and seventy-seven! Believe me, life is one long surprise. And you can't plan it, but you *can* prepare."

The List helps us all prepare. You might be turning thirty, as I was when I read it; you might be well past that birthday, or nowhere near. Either way, I hope the book it has spawned, full of rich observations by some of the most gifted women writers out there (including Maya Angelou herself), feeds your brain and your heart just as the original list fed mine, and then some.

Being a woman may be more complicated than ever, but DVRs and Diet Coke help. So will this book.

Happy birthday.

# 30 Things
Every Woman Should
*Have* and Should *Know*
by the Time She's 30

# Introduction

BY PAMELA REDMOND SATRAN,
AUTHOR OF THE "30 THINGS" LIST

On my thirtieth birthday, I refused to go to my own surprise party. With a full-time job (at *Glamour*) and a new baby, I was too exhausted to trek out to the restaurant where my husband had said only that we were having dinner. And my mother had recently died, leaving me not only grief-stricken but stunned by the power of my grief.

Plus, you know, I was freakin' *turning thirty*. All I wanted to do that night was crawl into bed and not get out.

My poor husband finally broke down and confessed that all our friends were waiting to celebrate my birthday. They'd been at the restaurant for more than an hour. Also, he argued, I was turning thirty! I deserved to have some fun!

Motivated more by shame than by any party spirit, I dried my tears, sucked it up, and wiggled into a formfitting vintage black dress that I hadn't worn since before I got pregnant. I slipped into my big-girl shoes and teetered up the street, buoyed by the prospect of turning the tables on my friends and surprising *them* by being unsurprised, dressed up, and ready to party.

I remember two things about that thirtieth birthday party that nearly wasn't.

The first is that I had a wonderful time. As beleaguered as I felt on so many levels, I was able to let it all go that night and revel in my friends, my neighborhood, my marriage—in the adult life I'd spent more than a decade building. So what that I was exhausted? I had a gorgeous baby girl and a job I loved. My adorable husband had transcended his own exhaustion to arrange this party. Yes, I was sad about my mother, but her death had brought me closer to my father and my brother, and that night my friends surrounded me with support and love.

And—I'm sorry, but this element of the evening was not unimportant—I fit back into that bitchin' dress!!

Wearing it again made me realize that no matter how huge the changes I'd been through, I was still the same person at thirty that I'd been at twenty-seven and fifteen and nine. And would be (I can now attest to the truth of this) at thirty-eight and forty-four and beyond.

Turning thirty was not reaching a pinnacle, after which everything would slide downhill. That birthday was just a particularly vivid dot on the straight line of my existence.

But it's true that something shifted that night.

I say that because the other thing I remember about that party is its intense Before-and-After quality.

Before was standing in my kitchen, half-dressed in my pajamas, crying, refusing to go out to dinner. And After was walking into the restaurant, wiggling my hips, throwing my arms up, and laughing.

Before was preparation: leaving home, going to college, launching a career, getting married, having a child, realizing that love might be forever but life was not. After was living with the choices I'd made: that man, that child, that profession, that city, that self.

Before was the end of my childhood. And After was the beginning of my full adult life.

Now, I don't want to insult anyone out there, including my daughter, the baby who was a newborn that night, by saying that you're not a grown-up until you turn thirty. You are—of course you are, with full privileges to play in the adults-only sandbox.

But for many of us there is a sense, whether it's justified or absurd, that throughout your twenties you are becoming—becoming someone and something that, once you turn thirty, you simply *are*.

I was meditating heavily on all this when I wrote "30 Things Every Woman Should Have and Should Know by the Time She's 30." It was 1997, and I'd been writing the Glamour List, a column I launched in *Glamour* magazine, for a couple of years by that point. Reader response to the column had been overwhelmingly positive and inspiring, and it was clear women wanted the Glamour List to move far beyond throw-away quips about sex and guys: They wanted actual wisdom they could grow into and refer back to for years to come.

My thirtieth birthday was well behind me by the time I wrote the column. But I still envisioned thirty—in my own life, in my friends' lives, in life in general—as a kind of train station. At that station, you got off the train you'd been riding up to that time, the train that had your parents on it, your siblings and your school friends, your textbooks and your pink diary with the lock and key—everything that had been trailing behind you for your entire life. And you got ready to board a different train, a train that would take you the rest of the way.

Once you got off the first train but before you climbed onto the second one, you had to make sure you had certain things—some material things, but mostly things in your heart and in your mind. Things you'd learned along the way, maybe without even realizing it. Ideas worth saving from childhood and ideas you needed to toss out the window.

For many women, reaching this juncture doesn't happen on the day they turn thirty, maybe not even during that symbolic year. It might come at twenty-eight or thirty-five; it might be pegged not to an age but to a life event, like a job promotion or a major move. You may even make the transition without realizing it until months or years later.

When I wrote this list, I thought of everything I'd fought to have and to know by the time I was thirty, things that had proven valuable in my journey toward and beyond that age. I also included all the things I *wished* I'd had and known by thirty. I felt, in the end, that I'd put together a really good list: smart and funny, practical and inspirational. I believed (still do) it was one of the best and truest things I'd written. *Glamour* published it, readers loved it—and then I moved on. Literally moved, in fact, across the country, from New Jersey to California, with my young family, getting my kids settled in school and going back to school myself to follow my longtime dream of writing novels.

Two or three years passed. And then, one morning, I opened an email forward from a friend. She usually didn't pass these things on, she wrote, but this one was so fabulous she just couldn't resist. All her girlfriends absolutely had to read it and follow the advice therein.

The title of the email she forwarded—"Things Every Woman Should Have and Should Know"—sounded awfully familiar. My name wasn't on it, nor was *Glamour*'s. As I read the items, I at first thought the writer had borrowed heavily from one of my lists. Then I realized this *was* my list: every last little bit of it, forwarded to and by what was in those pre-Facebook days an astounding number of women. One of them had retyped The List and sent it to ten of her friends, who sent it to ten of their friends; by the time it reached my inbox, there were hundreds of cc's. Before there was even a term for it, The List had gone viral.

I remember my face turning hot with the dawning realization that these were my exact words. I fired back a Reply All: *I wrote this! Please pass it on and say that it came from Glamour!*

Done, I figured. But I was wrong. The List *kept* turning up—again and again and, wow, again. In the months and years that followed, it landed in my inbox dozens of times and began appearing on websites as well, attributed to "Anonymous" or to authors as diverse as Hillary Clinton and Jesse Jackson and Maya Angelou. To my shock, my work was labeled "Maya Angelou's Best Poem Ever." (Thank you!) And every time I'd Google "cordless drill + black lace bra," I'd get about a thousand new search results.

I finally decided to set the record straight. I wrote a piece for *Glamour* about the phenomenon and blogged about The List's second life for the Huffington Post. But none of that stopped The List, which continued on its independent voyage around the globe.

And oh, the places it's gone! It's been . . .

- delivered to Serbian schoolteachers in honor of Mother's Day,
- taught in a Mississippi elementary school writing program,
- distributed as inspiration to battered women,
- turned into a quilt by artist Celeste Janey,

- championed by *French Women Don't Get Fat* author Mireille Guiliano, who recommended it to her fans "from ages 22 to 82 and beyond,"
- posted on the wall of a bar near Australia's Great Barrier Reef, where I am invited for a drink on the house anytime,
- and used as a character's dying words—dying words, people!—on a BBC radio play.

One of the hundreds of emails I've gotten from lovers of The List (who've made hundreds of my days) read: "I am possibly the last woman on earth to have read the 'best poem ever' and loved it! I'd like to thank *you* for writing such a meaningful and profound poem . . . it has opened my eyes and came at a time when I needed it the most." Another came from an Iraqi teenager, who wrote to ask if she could translate it into Kurdish. (We said, "Of course!") I've heard from women at halfway houses who were looking for hope and found a little in The List. Even my own daughter tells me it's making the rounds of her twentysomething friends.

I am awed, in the true sense of the word, by not just how *many* women but how many *different kinds* of women The List has touched. And now, of course, it's become this book, my original thirty sentences spun out into thousands of words of wisdom by some of the women I most admire. Writer Kelly Corrigan meditates on why every woman should have one friend who makes her laugh and one who lets her cry, and comedian Kathy Griffin puts her own hilarious spin on when to try harder and when to walk away. ZZ Packer talks about why you should have a youth you're content to move beyond, and Suze Orman and Katie Couric expand on what to do once you've traveled past thirty. Even Maya Angelou contributed—see page 163 for that!

The funny thing is, all these years later, I find myself *still* feeling as if I need to have and to know everything on this list, which I guess is why it's resonated so widely for so long. This is not a scorecard so much as a reminder of what we all should aim for and appreciate in our own lives, whether thirty is still a point on our horizon or has become a distant memory, whether we're planning for our future or living, as we all do, in the vivid and ageless everyday.

I may not have started out on some grand mission to illuminate this important life passage for women, but with *Glamour* behind me, that's where I ended up. Just like that night of my thirtieth birthday, when I thought I was heading straight to bed and found myself instead in a lively room, wearing a tight dress, surrounded by love and possibilities. Just like we all start out believing we're going one place, only to find ourselves, at those great train stations of life, having arrived at quite another, unimaginably better place.

So take this list not as a destination but as a launching point. Explore the insights ahead, embrace what speaks to you, ignore what doesn't, and let yourself be swayed by the beat of your own heart. Sure, every woman should have and should know everything on this list. But how you come to know and have it, and when, and why, and with whom—that's what you alone can bring to it. That's the magic.

And now, the list that's inspired, comforted, tickled, and challenged thousands of women, to love, share, and make your own.

# 30 Things Every Woman
## *Know* by the

### *By 30, you should have . . .*

1. One old boyfriend you can imagine going back to and one who reminds you of how far you've come.

2. A decent piece of furniture not previously owned by anyone else in your family.

3. Something perfect to wear if the employer or man of your dreams wants to see you in an hour.

4. A purse, a suitcase, and an umbrella you're not ashamed to be seen carrying.

5. A youth you're content to move beyond.

6. A past juicy enough that you're looking forward to retelling it in your old age.

7. The realization that you are actually going to *have* an old age— and some money set aside to help fund it.

8. An email address, a voice mailbox, and a bank account— all of which nobody has access to but you.

9. A résumé that is not even the slightest bit padded.

10. One friend who always makes you laugh and one who lets you cry.

11. A set of screwdrivers, a cordless drill, and a black lace bra.

12. Something ridiculously expensive that you bought for yourself, just because you deserve it.

13. The *belief* that you deserve it.

14. A skin-care regimen, an exercise routine, and a plan for dealing with those few other facets of life that don't get better after 30.

15. A solid start on a satisfying career, a satisfying relationship, and all those other facets of life that *do* get better.

# Should *Have* and Should
# Time She's 30

## By 30, you should know . . .

1. How to fall in love without losing yourself.

2. How you feel about having kids.

3. How to quit a job, break up with a man, and confront a friend without ruining the friendship.

4. When to try harder and when to walk away.

5. How to kiss in a way that communicates perfectly what you would and wouldn't like to happen next.

6. The names of the secretary of state, your great-grandmothers, and the best tailor in town.

7. How to live alone, even if you don't like to.

8. Where to go—be it your best friend's kitchen table or a yoga mat—when your soul needs soothing.

9. That you can't change the length of your legs, the width of your hips, or the nature of your parents.

10. That your childhood may not have been perfect, but it's over.

11. What you would and wouldn't do for money or love.

12. That nobody gets away with smoking, drinking, doing drugs, or not flossing for very long.

13. Who you can trust, who you can't, and why you shouldn't take it personally.

14. Not to apologize for something that isn't your fault.

15. Why they say life begins at 30!

By 30, you

should have ...

**1** One old boyfriend you can imagine going back to and one who reminds you of how far you've come.

## BY GENEVIEVE FIELD

I'M ABOUT TO MAKE A BIG PROMISE: THIS ITEM, THE very first on The List, can bring you lasting happiness in love, and self-acceptance, too.

Of course, I only know so in retrospect, which is too bad because I really could've used a little love wisdom back in 2001, when I was thirty-one and guiltily wearing a diamond-studded platinum engagement ring I feared I didn't deserve. I was tortured about love back then, in part because of my rocky romantic history; if you'd told me then that that history had made me a *better* person, not a less love-worthy one, I'd have told you to have another drink.

I'd been in a couple healthy relationships, sure. There was even a high school sweetheart I sometimes thought of as my Mr. Almost—a lanky, towheaded basketball player I could've ended up marrying in an alternate universe where only his kindness and hotness and devotion to me (*not* his political views, antithetical to mine) mattered. But since then I'd had high-drama and often misguided relationships, and now I was having real doubts that I could be the happily-ever-after bride my fiancé, Ted, saw in me.

It wasn't that I was having doubts about *him*. I was crazy about Ted, had fought off a bunch of art-school babes for him. After all, he was funny, sensitive, wildly creative, and he had the softest brown-eyed gaze I'd ever stared into. So yes, I longed to start a life with this man and, yes, to have his babies. And yet lately I'd been staying up later than him, sometimes hours later, lying in the dark on the sofa in our tiny apartment, watching the shadows of a gingko tree flutter on our white brick walls. I told myself it wasn't getting married I was worried about; it was everything else. It *had* been an epic year. I'd quit (with a fair share of attitude and no parachute) a big-deal job at a business I'd cofounded with my now ex; I'd had a cancer scare and contemplated my own mortality for the first time; the World Trade Center had been attacked (and was still smoldering less than a mile away from our home); and I was planning my wedding.

"Genny, come to bed!" Ted would whisper from the other side of the bookshelf that separated our "bedroom" from our "living room." And I would. And he would take off my tank top and press his beating heart against mine and I would feel better—until about 3 a.m., that is, when I'd awaken from some apocalyptic dream in a clammy sweat, thinking those thoughts again: *What if I can't control the future of my marriage any more than I can control the future of this planet? What if I have a midlife crisis and cheat on Ted the way Married cheated on his wife—with me?*

Oh, let me tell you about Married. He's *my* version of The List's "one who reminds you of how far you've come." He'd been out of my life for eight years by the time I got engaged (I'd been in college when we had whatever it was we had), but he'd been weighing heavily on my mind ever since Ted and I decided to marry. God, in school I'd been obsessed with him—this married older man who acted anything *but* married. He said his wife had fallen out of love with him and was probably seeing someone else too. I accepted this justification unquestioningly, then split ways with my disapproving roommates and rented my own place so I could be alone with him every opportunity we, or rather he, got. He would only come after dark, hiding his motorcycle in the bamboo thicket outside my fence and glancing over his shoulder as he crossed my threshold. (Did I hate the secrecy or thrive on it? I think both. Isn't it always both?) He delivered his kisses like drugs, and I accepted them, swam in their chemical glow. It was only when he wasn't there that I thought about his wife. Where was my conscience as we sped through the rain on that bike, laughing? Where was my self-respect when I snapped at him to "stay with *me* tonight!"? Could I lose my bearings so easily again?

One evening, about a month before my wedding, I sat down with a new but close friend, Ashley, and recounted this ignoble chapter in my life: my inability to stop myself, Married's many lies, his wife's pain when she learned the truth. "Can I do this?" I asked Ash. "Can I be trusted with Ted's heart when I've been such a shit?"

My wise-beyond-her-years friend then said something I've never forgotten: "You can't change your past, but you *can* change your mind about your past."

I won't claim that a chorus of angels rang out and I instantly grasped the cosmic significance of what Ashley was saying. But I will say that from then on, as my wedding day zoomed into the almost-present and Ted and I made our last-minute decisions on lanterns, rehearsal dinner music, sparklers, guitar players, salad dressings, vows, and flowers, I began to feel better. Maybe I wasn't a terrible person, after all. Maybe I was just learning—like all of us—how to be good. I stopped waking at 3 a.m. to assail myself for my past misdeeds; no longer glanced down to find myself nervously twisting my engagement ring; and for the first time since I'd been wearing that ring, quit thinking of *any* man but the one who'd given it to me.

And I'm happy to report that when I took Ted's hand on

our wedding day and said I would stand by him till we got too old and creaky to stand up anymore, I knew I was woman enough—finally—to be true to my word.

Now, with nine years of marriage under my belt (plus my 20/20-hindsight contact lenses and a small collection of self-help books written by wise Tibetan guys with no possessions), I can tell you with at least 90 percent conviction that we are not doomed to repeat our mistakes—not if we've learned everything we can from them. Forgive your old self, and you can be pretty sure she will forgive you too.

One more thing those Buddhist monks like to say: Every relationship we have in our lives, whether it lasts five hours with a stranger on a plane or fifty years with our soulmate, is meant to teach us something. And ultimately, I think that's what this item on The List is about: It's not about the exes; it's about *you*. Will you cower in the shadows of your past or grow beyond them? Look back in anger or empathy? Me, I'm done regretting my time with Married. I learned *plenty* about love and about myself from him, but the greatest lesson was the most obvious: Love should almost never make you cry. If you've sobbed or had too many drinks or felt your stomach knot up over a guy more than once for every month you've been together, this is not the love you were meant to have. Thank him for the lessons and move on.

As for what I learned from that one old boyfriend I can

imagine going back to (in an alternate universe with no CNN to argue over and, of course, no Ted)? Well, it took me, ahem, twenty-five years to figure this one out, but here it is: I am a knock-down, drag-out Democrat whom even a red-blooded Republican could love; I must be one in a million.

**GENEVIEVE FIELD**, forty-one, is a contributing editor at *Glamour* and the cofounder of the online magazine and dating site Nerve. She is the editor of several anthologies of fiction and nonfiction, including *Sex and Sensibility: 28 True Romances from the Lives of Single Women*.

A decent piece of furniture not previously owned by anyone else in your family.

## BY SLOANE CROSLEY

I COME FROM A SMALL FAMILY. I DON'T MEAN numbers-wise, although it's true that we are a minor lot: just Mom and Dad and a couple of kids. I mean height-, weight-, history-, square-foot-, and carbon-footprint-wise—my family just doesn't take up that much space. If I opened my bedroom door, I had a nice view of the living room, the dining room, the kitchen, and the two other bedrooms in my home.

We weren't rich and we weren't poor. A little research and get-up-and-go might have resulted in a larger space. But as it is with most parents, mine are creatures of habit. They bought our house as a "starter home" and never left. It was the last major acquisition they made—and that included everything in it.

For Mom and Dad, "redecorating" meant a fresh coat of paint and a new matching toothbrush holder and tissue box

cover. I have absolutely no recollection of my parents volun-
tarily purchasing a single piece of new furniture in the thirty-
three years I have known them. Their living room sees one
new television set per decade. And it was only when the dining
room table cracked in half that they went out and bought a
new one—all-glass with beveled edges—as well as some high-
backed chairs covered in baby blue suede. Twenty-five years
later, imagining my parents' house without those dated chairs
is like imagining it without a roof.

Needless to say, when it came time for me to move into my
first apartment, my parents had nothing to give on the furniture front. Not a stitch or a stick that they weren't already using. In one way, this was symbolic of an efficiently lived and
environmentally sound life. These people were never in danger
of becoming hoarders. But in another way? It sucked. Most
newly minted graduates tend to have at least one piece they've
"had forever." A chair from their childhood bedroom or a lamp
from Grandma. This lifts both an emotional and a financial
burden. Or so I imagine it does. As for me, I spent my early
twenties purchasing boring, anonymous blond furniture because I had to have *something* and it was all I could afford.

But in my late twenties, something shifted. I would walk
into my apartment and feel somehow stunted. Wasn't this
headboard-free double bed supposed to be temporary?
When I'd bought my white "Ektorp" Ikea sofa, I'd vowed to

replace it after that first inevitable red wine spill; now it seemed depressingly permanent. Having never invested in a single piece of furniture I loved, did I even count as a grown-up?

As women, we experience our first major purchases as a kind of rite of passage. If we're lucky enough to have the opportunity to make a good living, we purchase a really nice designer handbag to tell the world, "I'm old enough to afford this." By the age of, say, twenty-seven, we find ourselves springing for nice dinners with girlfriends and taking vacations that necessitate airplanes. But by the time we're staring down the barrel of thirty, furniture really is the final frontier. The purchase of it (over a new dress) requires a shifting perspective, one that says, "I live here now." "Here" being your own life.

It was time for me to open my eyes, to stop becoming overly accustomed to my surroundings. If I didn't purchase a desk or a coffee table, I was going to turn into my parents.

One day, weary of searching, I stopped in front of a store that sells an expensive European makeup line. Quality makeup was actually the kind of purchase I was comfortable with then. (Twenty-dollar lip gloss I'll lose tomorrow? Naturally. A $200 lamp I'll own the rest of my life? I don't think so.) I had passed the store every day for years, but only now did I notice the green studded Victorian chair that somehow fit perfectly on a checkered tile floor. Thinking it couldn't hurt to ask, I approached a saleswoman inside, who gave me a phone number to call.

"This is the president of the company," she explained. "She buys all the chairs at estate sales in Europe. You can call and ask her."

The next thing I knew, I was awkwardly conveying my chair infatuation to a nice Swiss lady. She told me it was one-of-a-kind, having been carefully selected for the store after years of searching.

"However"—she paused, perhaps intrigued by the oddity of the call—"I can sell it to you for five hundred dollars if you promise me you'll give it a good home."

I gulped upon hearing the price, immediately reverting back to the comfort of an earlier mind-set, calculating how much more practical it would be to spend that money on dinners. Plus, spring was coming—didn't I need a trench coat or some open-toed shoes or something?

But I had gotten this far. I loved that chair. I wanted that chair. It was less like the old me and everything like the person I wanted to become: a person comfortable enough in her own life to sit and stay awhile.

I knew the answer to her question. I could most certainly give it a good home. It would, in fact, be the first and only unique thing of value there. Besides me, of course. Now, when I look at the chair, it has a firstborn feel to it. I've acquired a handful of other decent pieces of furniture over time, but it's the chair that always gets the most compliments, the chair that every single guest has naturally gravitated toward when walking through my front door. Now all I have to do is keep the red wine away from it.

---

**SLOANE CROSLEY**, thirty-three, is the author of the books *I Was Told There'd Be Cake* and *How Did You Get This Number.* She is a frequent contributor to *The New York Times* and other publications.

Something perfect to wear if the employer or man of your dreams wants to see you in an hour.

## BY ANNE CHRISTENSEN

OF ALL THE ITEMS ON THIS LIST, THIS HAS ALWAYS been my very favorite. Possibly because it's one I *know* I've got down! And you should, too, because life is a lot easier when you're not dashing around in a panic over what you're going to wear to some hugely important thing that's happening seven and a half minutes from now. Allow me to give you my list of twelve wardrobe staples every woman should own. It's like CliffsNotes for your closet!

1. **Skinny black jeans.** You need a pair. Dress them up for the office or down for day.

2. **A crisp, white button-down shirt.** It suggests clean, cool confidence in the workplace, but unbutton two buttons and it's the ultimate in sex appeal for night.

**3. A go-to dress.** It doesn't have to be a little black dress. It's even better sometimes if it's *not*, because color makes a bolder statement. But it should fit perfectly and make you feel beautiful.

**4. A classic black pump.** It has to have at least a four-inch heel to boost your height *and* confidence. (Okay, fine. A three-inch heel if you must.)

**5. A bright mini.** My own favorite is red with a flared hem. It's great to have one that's a really bright color because it makes you stand out in a crowd. You can wear it for day—just pair it with an oversize men's white sweater—or nighttime, with a silk camisole.

**6. A bold piece of jewelry.** Think: necklace, bangle, large ring, large earrings. I have a big necklace that I keep in my drawer at work, and it dresses up any outfit. A statement piece allows your personal style to shine, especially if the rest of your outfit is conservative.

**7. A fitted blazer.** A great-fitting blazer is a girl's most invaluable staple. Pop the collar, roll the sleeves, or add a cool brooch to make it your own.

**8. A colorful clutch.** This one's especially crucial if you have a closet full of blacks or neutrals. A splash of color will liven up the simplest outfit—not to mention your mood.

**9. Black opaque tights.** They're so warm and practical, and they instantly make a dress look professional.

**10. A lace tank.** Wear it underneath your V-neck during the day or peeking out from under a jacket in the evening.

**11. Ballet flats.** They're feminine and comfortable, and you can wear them anywhere and always look pulled together. I personally love a blue ballet flat.

**12. A soft, luxurious white T-shirt.** It has to be a great-quality one that feels good on your skin. You can wear it with everything else in your wardrobe. And if you find one you *really* love, buy three.

---

**ANNE CHRISTENSEN**, forty-five, is the executive fashion director of *Glamour*. She has also served as fashion director of *The New York Times' T Magazine*, and her styling has been featured in the American, Italian, and Chinese editions of *Vogue*.

you're not ashamed to be seen carrying.

5

A youth you're content
to move beyond.

## BY ZZ PACKER

WHEN I THINK BACK TO THE TIME IN MY LIFE WHEN
I was the most joyful and wild, young and free, I think of Baltimore. I lived there in my early twenties, a fledgling writer and high school teacher who was only four years older than my oldest student. I was so young I still listened to the same music as my pupils. I'd drive down rowhouse-lined Calvert Street, blasting Wu-Tang Clan and Soundgarden in endless rotation, my little silver Toyota Corolla an echo chamber, each song reminding me that there was something thrilling, sad, romantic, and vaguely debaucherous about being young and alive.

And when I think of Baltimore, I can't help but think of my first love. I met him at a party where he was clamping jumper cables to himself and daring others to do the same. Of course, no one else did. Crazy, I took him up on it, and left the jumper cable teeth on my fingers for a full minute, determined not to appear weak. I was like that then—if someone said Japanese was difficult, I would sign up for a year of it, then work three jobs to afford a summer in Tokyo. I learned how to drive by going cross-country with a friend, whom I'd had the temerity to ask, the day before heading out, "Okay, so which is the brake and which is the accelerator?" Needless to say, a guy who dared me to attach jumper cables to myself—and who'd give $5 to the homeless when he himself might only have another fifteen in his bank account—instantly had my heart.

We soon rented a place together in what used to be an honest-to-God mansion but was now split into apartments. It was beautiful, gigantic, and, at $325 apiece, startlingly cheap—probably because at any given hour, a trio of drug dealers could be found hawking their wares just outside the entrance. I came from a family of religious, straitlaced black Southerners and had been raised to be cautious and afraid of the world, but, at twenty-four, I wasn't afraid anymore. I thought it couldn't get better than being in love with someone and huddling together on the stoop while the older neighbors shook their heads; or hurtling down the city streets on the way to some hipster lounge, where I'd sit under dim red lights and squint at pages of stories that would never get published. I was forever marveling at the world. Every song was a soundtrack to whatever emotion I was feeling, every day a new chapter to a book in which I was the heroine.

Back then, even the most mundane activities held a special charm. Buying groceries was playing grown-up; taking the train to D.C. to visit my boyfriend's parents was a bona fide adventure. When we arrived, grinning like crazy, they would treat us to dinner at a favorite Lebanese place, followed by a movie.

Of course, my boyfriend and I broke up and got back together more times than I can count, and they were always hormonal, operatic breakups, usually beginning with the angrier party driving halfway across the country with the other in pursuit. It didn't matter where we were going. Each and every direction was a possibility.

But time, as I came to learn, only moves in one direction, and somewhat reluctantly, I traveled with it: The boyfriend and I parted paths; I fell in love again, got married, had kids, and found myself listening to less rap, more soulful guys on guitars. Then one morning two years ago, I got a phone call. My ex-boyfriend, my former partner in crime, had suddenly, tragically died. I flew to visit his parents as soon as I could. Though the occasion was obviously sad, I loved seeing his mom and dad, and the flood of old memories engulfed me once again. "I remember we saw that Marlon Riggs film at the Key Theatre," I told them as we drove past the place—or, later, "You took us to Lebanese Taverna all the time."

"Oh," his mother said. "I guess we did." They seemed touched but also a little sad that I'd remembered something they'd probably forgotten, or only remembered once I'd said it. That's when I realized I'd been holding on to something they'd let go of long before, and that their son, before he died, had lived a new life, consumed with marriage, fatherhood, his life as a writer, then as a lawyer—all more important events than the ones I'd trapped in amber.

I realized part of me still longed to be back there, in the Baltimore of my memories—back on that roller coaster, that wild free ride I would line up to do again and again. I had come to think of my twenties as the very best, most exciting time in my life, a time that couldn't be topped; I'd begun to mythologize the past.

But now I don't.

Not because it's not worth cherishing memories, but because we are molting, shedding, metamorphosing creatures. Most of us fear that in growing old, we'll become a shell of ourselves. But, of course, it's the youthful versions of ourselves that are our shells; we must leave them behind like a snakeskin. We must grow out of ourselves to grow beyond our old limits, or else risk being suffocated by the sediment of our own history. Stopping time, I understood after my visit, was not only impossible; it wasn't even desirable.

I now believe in growing old gratefully, not gracefully. I haven't found the secret to life, or love, or eternal youth. But

I do know now that youth is not the blossom but the bud, and that though one cannot always be young and wild, if you are willing to learn, to grow, to outrun the mileposts of your own wildest dreams, you can always be winsome and lucky, lovely and free.

**ZZ PACKER**, thirty-nine, was named one of *The New Yorker*'s "20 Under 40." She is the author of the story collection *Drinking Coffee Elsewhere.*

# What 30 means to me

## BY TAYLOR SWIFT

### HAVING NO DEADLINES FOR LOVE OR ANYTHING ELSE

I've been thinking about turning thirty—and forty and fifty!—since I was about ten. I've always wondered what I'll feel like at those ages, and I spend a lot of time daydreaming about the future.

Hopefully, at thirty, I'll be like my friend and fiddle player Caitlin. Everyone thinks she's twenty-three, but she's thirty-two. She's just this carefree little hippie. Once, I asked her how she felt about getting older, and she said, "I'm never going to." She lives her life like *I'm never going to act burdened and bitter and all the things that make people seem older than they are.* Caitlin is also the kind of person who doesn't fall in love often, but when she does, she falls in love love love *love.*

I guess I'm already like Caitlin in that way. It's rare that

I have a boyfriend—that only happens if I fall in love. I've noticed that people who are never in a relationship *just* to be in a relationship keep their childlike spark because they don't end up settling for things that make them unhappy, and they never feel as if they took less than what was out there for them. So for me, being single is what I do, and falling in love is the exception.

Lately I've been listening to "You Learn" by Alanis Morissette: "You live, you learn. You love, you learn. You cry, you learn. You lose, you learn." I think there's something pretty comforting in knowing that even the biggest mistakes I'm inevitably going to make will turn me into who I'll be at thirty.

One thing I've learned in my twenties is that if a relationship has to be kept secret, you shouldn't be in it. Going forward, that's going to be a concrete, 100-percent-of-the-time rule for me. If a guy wants to keep the relationship quiet—whether it's some weird privacy thing or he just doesn't want to show you off—and if you don't feel the same way, and it makes you feel like he's not proud of you, then that's not the relationship you want to be in.

Another rule of thumb is that if it doesn't *feel* like love—if you're sad more than you're happy—that's a huge indicator that you need to walk. You need to know when to let go.

For now, I have absolutely no love plans for thirty. No deadlines. Just vague, blurry, pretty daydreams. You never know what's going to happen. I do hope that marriage and children are in my future. I think it would be unbelievable someday to be chasing around a couple of crazy little kids who have tangled hair and mismatched clothing because we let them dress themselves. One of them would be in a princess costume, and the other kid would walk around in a Spider-Man suit because he wanted to, and we wouldn't bother arguing with him.

With daydreams like that, it's almost impossible to fear turning *any* milestone age.

**TAYLOR SWIFT**, twenty-two, released her first (multiplatinum) album at sixteen, had the best-selling album of 2009 at nineteen, and won four Grammys, including Album of the Year, at twenty. *Speak Now*, her third album, went triple-platinum-plus. In 2010 she was the top-selling digital artist in music history.

A past juicy enough that you're looking forward to retelling it in your old age.

**BY AYANA BYRD**

AT FIFTEEN, I WAS NOT THE GIRL YOU'D COME TO FOR a juicy story. I was the girl who *meant* to cut a day of high school but never got around to it before graduating fourth in my class; who needed to be sure—absolutely sure—I was in love with my boyfriend before we would, one day, have sex (no matter that my friends had been doing it with half of Philadelphia for years).

I never minded being the good girl, because I had friends who showed me that too wild a time could come with serious consequences. Like Emily, whom I met in freshman homeroom but got to know at keg parties. By eighteen, she'd gone to rehab three times for cocaine, gotten out, discovered heroin, and died from an overdose. Emily was my teenage reminder that there is a rock bottom that you can hit, even if you are young and beautiful and smart and loved. She symbolized the reasons I stayed far from the edge, enjoying the safety of the middle.

But the middle wasn't taking me anywhere. I especially remember feeling this way at one Grateful Dead concert, as I watched my friends whirl around in colorful Indian-print skirts, looking as if they were connecting with something important. I wanted to step outside myself too, to be just as loose—but minus the acid that had gotten them there.

Soon after the concert, I was asked to spend a year in Belgium as an exchange student. And so, as my friends back home experimented with sex, drugs, and shoplifting, I found my own addiction: traveling.

The truth is that the Belgian trip began with me begging the flight attendant to let me off the plane. I'd never flown before, never left my mother for more than a week. *This was a mistake.* When we landed eight hours later, though, my perspective had already begun to shift. I wasn't going back home; I was going to be uncomfortable and sink into this French- and Flemish-speaking unknown. *This was not the middle.*

Since that scary, amazing year, I haven't stopped seeking adventure. To date, I've traveled to four continents, twenty-six countries, and most of the fifty states. So while I've never had a one-night stand or danced on a table with the after-work crowd, I have fallen in love with someone I met on a bridge in Florence and done the salsa with a seventy-three-year-old Cuban man in a Havana bar. I've sacrificed job security in exchange for the freedom to hop on a plane at a moment's notice, but I've never minded because these stories and the lasting friendships that have grown out of them are my treasures. One day, many years from now, I will pass them along to my children and their children. I will tell them . . .

**Everyone has an inner Cyrano de Bergerac.** Apparently, my Eurail pass did not cover travel through war-torn Croatia. As my Vienna-bound train zoomed through the desolate, pitch-black countryside at 3 a.m., the conductor demanded money to cover the miles. I had dollars and an AmEx; he wanted Croatian currency or MasterCard. Unamused, he pointed outside, letting me know I was going to have to disembark. "Isn't there a war still going on?!" I asked. "Do you have daughters?" my best friend pleaded with the man. No daughters, no sympathy . . . except from three Romanian men, fellow passengers, who paid our way in exchange for us penning a love letter to a British woman one of them liked. We wrote until the sun came up, filled with a gratitude that we hoped translated to passion on paper.

**The sunrise looks better with elephants.** Because I never say no to a trip, I once traveled to South Africa with only $147 in my wallet. There, I got to sit in Nelson Mandela's old jail cell, talk to women my age who were girls under apartheid, and start my twenty-seventh birthday on a safari, watching elephants walk with their babies at dawn. Three experiences it's safe to say I'll *never* have in Brooklyn.

**She who is ugly in Morocco is beautiful in Italy.** Walking through a crowded souk in Marrakech, a man mocked me in unsure English, "Ugh . . . too skinny!" Weeks before, his dismissal would have ruined my afternoon. Now I shrugged, remembering how two days prior, this same size 2 had gotten cheers of *"Bellissima!"* on the cobblestoned streets of Rome. It's useless to obsess over one standard of beauty, since it can change as soon as you cross a border. My travels have taught me this: The world can't decide what's beautiful. So *you* decide, okay?

**Old Hungarian ladies know something about aging that most women don't.** The attendant at the bathhouse in Budapest did not give out towels, no matter how many times I asked. Therefore, my bare butt was on display in the hot bath, the cold pool, and the steam room full of women who were on average sixty years older than me. I felt embarrassed—but these ladies with their wrinkles, stretch marks, and sags seemed perfectly self-confident naked. Only later, fully dressed, did I ask myself, *How am I going to one day feel good about a body that showed its age if I am ashamed of the twenty-three-year-old one I have now?* Today, when insecurity strikes, I think of those women and keep my head high.

**Some things suck. But you recover.** Once, on a single day in Barcelona, at least five men called me *puta* (that's "whore") after I ignored their advances on the street. That was my second-worst travel experience ever. The worst: eating a bad salad in Bogotá and spending the next twenty-four hours wrapped around a toilet—while the wedding of a dear friend happened without me. Guess what? It all passes. I got through those bummers with a hardiness I hadn't known I possessed. And I came out on the other side, not more afraid of life's poisonous moments but less so. What I couldn't have known was that the trials I'd faced abroad were preparing me for ones I'd inevitably face back home.

Sometimes when a trip ends, one you hadn't planned begins. After two weeks traipsing around Portugal, I landed at New York's JFK airport, checked voice mail outside of customs, and rushed to the hospital. There, my twenty-six-year-old boyfriend of five years lay weakly as doctors guessed what was wrong with his lungs. I did everything I could for Dayvon, many times squeezing next to him in his tiny hospital bed so he wouldn't have to spend the night alone. But it didn't help. Nothing helped. Six weeks later, he died from an autoimmune disease, Wegener's granulomatosis. I always say I was one woman before his death and have been another ever since. The one before thought she could fix anything if she just worked hard enough. The woman after was forced to accept that sometimes life has plans for us and our loved ones that are far, far beyond our grasp.

After Dayvon died, I felt the middle calling me back. I wanted to retreat so I wouldn't have to face my hurt, and the outside world was newly daunting without his presence in it. So I threw myself into planning a twenty-fifth-birthday party, hoping that the people I loved would gather in my house and fix me when I was too devastated to fix myself. At the end of the night, I went to bed and they cleaned up for me, blew out the candles. I woke up to a note: "For once, don't be good—there's *lots* of cake left, eat it all."

I did. And I stayed out of the middle. I kept traveling. Sitting in a certain *plaça* in Barcelona or sipping wine with a particular person in Paris reminds me that a Philly-born, Barnard-graduated Brooklyn girl is only a sliver of who I am and what defines me. In these places and moments, I feel limitless.

If the means to a well-lived life is to take the road less traveled, first you have to get on the road. I got on mine nearly kicking and screaming during a rainy flight to Belgium. And the road has saved me.

---

**AYANA BYRD**, thirty-eight, has found time between jaunts abroad to coauthor *Hair Story: Untangling the Roots of Black Hair in America* and coedit *Naked: Black Women Bare All About Their Hair, Skin, Hips, Lips, and Other Parts*. She has also been an articles editor at *Glamour* and written for *Rolling Stone* and *Essence* magazines.

7

The realization that you are actually going to *have* an old age—and some money set aside to help fund it.

**BY SUZE ORMAN**

OF ALL THE THINGS WOMEN SHOULD HAVE AND KNOW by the time they're thirty, here's one I believe in so completely that I want to help you put it into action. I know from experience that when you feel as if you can't control your money, it weighs on every part of your life. And when you *do* have your financial act together, you feel powerful, beautiful, and sexy. What could be better than that? These five rules will help you get there.

1. **Come clean about money.** It's easy to say, "Let's go out. I'll put it on my card." It's hard to muster up the courage to say, "I can't go out to eat because my credit card is almost maxed out." But here's the thing: It's not right to spend money you don't have to perpetuate a lie about who you are. I know a woman who was an executive at a major company when she was in her thirties. She rose up quickly, dressed beautifully,

seemed poised and together. And then she confessed to me that she had $150,000 of credit card debt that nobody knew about—not her boyfriend whom she lived with at the time, not her parents, not her friends. She was miserable, but she kept living this lie because she was expected to have money. I saw her recently—she's now in her forties—and she looked younger than she did the first time I met her. Turns out she took my advice and decided to come clean to the people she loved, and it helped her to start moving forward with her life and pay off her debt. By the time you're thirty, you should be able to face your financial truth head-on.

## 2. Give *to* yourself as much as you give of yourself.

Women in particular tend to give, give, give—to their friends, their significant other, their spouse, their kids, their pets, their plants—even to strangers on the street. But before you spend on anyone else, you need to put away money every single month, until you have an eight-month emergency fund. You need to pay off any credit card debt you have. You need to pay your bills on time. You need to start saving for retirement. Yes, that's a lot of stuff to check off a list, but it's important for your financial—and emotional—well-being.

The hard truth is that we're living in uncertain times. Medicare, Medicaid, Social Security—not all of those programs are going to be there for you the same way they are for your grandparents, so we have to be more responsible about our finances than ever. Young women say to me, "Suze, I can't save for retirement. I can't even afford to pay my bills." Here's the question: If you can't afford to pay your bills while you have a paycheck coming in, how are you going to pay for those exact same bills when you don't? The answer is, you're not going to be able to. Ensuring your financial future should be your number-one priority.

**3. Know how to ask for a raise and get it.** So many women put themselves on the sale rack—they never ask for what they're worth, and they always settle for less. But you have to realize that if you undervalue who you are, the world will undervalue you, too. By the time you're thirty, you should know how to ask for a raise and get it. First, you must know why you deserve a raise (and "Because I want more money" is not a good reason!). Then you go in and you sell yourself. When I was studying to be a financial advisor at Merrill Lynch in 1980, they taught me how to be a professional salesperson. They had me make one hundred calls a day to get people to buy something, and they said, "You are never to call somebody up and just say, 'Would you like to buy five hundred shares of IBM?'" Instead, I was to ask, "Would you like to buy five hundred or one thousand shares of IBM?" And just about every time— because few people have the ability to say, "Neither, what's the matter with you?"—they'd say, "Five hundred." Same philosophy applies when you're asking for a raise. You don't ask;

you tell. You say, "This is how I have impacted your company in the past six months or year. I have added this to the bottom line, I have gained these clients, I have launched these programs. Therefore, I would like either a 10 percent or 15 percent increase in my salary." You are never to ask a yes-or-no question about a raise.

**4. Live below your means but above your needs.** If you own a car, and the car works fine, but you want to buy a new car simply because you have the means to do so, don't! Keep the wheels you have for now. So many young women think that if they have any money, they should spend it. And I've realized that this is often because they are angry at money. They've got student loans that they'll be paying for years and years, they hate their job because they're not being paid what they're worth, real estate is still not affordable, and so what do they do? They spend money, thinking, *This will make me feel better.* But it won't unless they've saved for it—unless the money is there. Trust me, there's no better feeling than the pride you'll experience when you see your bank account growing every month and every year.

**5. Be your own financial advisor.** Here is what every woman needs to understand: Nobody is going to care about your money more than you do. Your financial success directly affects the quality of your life. Not my life, not your financial advisor's life, not your banker's life, but *your* life. Look at how many financial advisors and mortgage brokers told people that they should buy a home with no money down. It is the financial industry that brought down the world economy in 2008. And you're going to listen to these people and trust them to tell you what to do with your money? No—and I don't want to hear the excuse that money is too confusing.

Listen, I was a waitress making $400 a month until I was thirty. Some of my customers took a liking to me and gave me $50,000 to open up my own restaurant. They told me to put it in a money market account in a brokerage firm and keep it there until they could help me open the restaurant.

Well, I did that, and the broker was crooked, and in three months all that money was gone. That really lit a fire in me. I thought, *I could do better with my money than this.* So I got a job at Merrill Lynch, and my career was born. That's why I am who I am today, instead of a failed restaurateur. Women, I'm telling you: You have what it takes!

**SUZE ORMAN**, sixty, is the two-time Emmy Award–winning host of *The Suze Orman Show*. She is a sought-after motivational speaker and the author of *The Money Class*, among other best-selling financial advice books.

**8**

An email address, a voice mailbox, and a bank account—all of which nobody has access to but you.

## BY JACQUELYN MITCHARD

ONE OF THE BEST PIECES OF ADVICE I'VE EVER RE-ceived was from my grandmother, who said, "A woman always has to keep something of her own, even if it's a jar of quarters." The other was from my agent, another wise woman, who told me twenty years ago: "You don't have to tell everything you know."

Once upon a time, however, I used to do just that. In my twenties, life was an open house—literally and metaphorically. Mere acquaintances crashed on the couch for weeks on end. I opened my heart to any suitor who'd stick around long enough to learn my last name. And my women friends—well, they were enormously fun, gratuitously pretty, as wild as half-broke horses, and about as circumspect as ballistic missiles. For their entertainment, I dramatized racy details from my dating life, in which I usually regretted everything after the appetizers. Why did I make my private life so public? Maybe

I believed that the only way to be "genuine" was to lay bare every secret. I doled out wedges of myself in hopes that I would receive loyalty in return. But some things should be yours and yours alone. I realized that bartering privacy makes you poorer, while holding on to it and your most intimate thoughts can make you more intriguing, more powerful. There's no such thing as telling someone a secret: It stops being a secret the minute it's told. And if you're lucky, the older you get, the more you realize the blessing of boundaries.

How did I come to value mine? There was this older writer I'd known for years who made her reputation writing achingly personal essays—tales of midnight hookups in European subways, body-sculpting surgery, her regret over her son's passive-bystander role in a crime. People adored her, personally and professionally, and made pilgrimages to her house; she verged on being a cult figure. But one can only dance on the tabletops for so long without slipping on a puddle of beer. One of the casualties of telling too much about yourself is that you have to tell too much about the people closest to you as well. And my writer friend finally did. After she published a particularly intimate recollection of her divorce and its toll on her children, I watched the writer's family turn away from her for good. Their secrets were not safe with her.

By then I was thirty, a young mom and a professional writer, no longer a solo pilot. To love my young children and my husband, I really did have to love myself, too. The first step was to *build* a self, contemplating and gathering up all those pieces I'd once scattered around so freely. Second, I installed an editor—on my mouth. No longer was I the first to confide the grisly details of a marital fight or my kid's latest triumph. In fact, I established a conscious five-to-one ratio for listening versus telling. One evening, my school-aged cousin came to dinner and began telling us about a famous songwriter who'd visited her class that day. I was about to tell her that, when I was twenty and he was forty, I'd had a date with that songwriter. But then I shut my mouth. I'd wanted to seem impressive and important to my cousin but realized that my anecdote would have the exact opposite effect—no one finds a braggart wise. And once I no longer thought of listening as "waiting to talk," I began to have more meaningful conversations.

I took the next step. I found a modest wooden box, about the size of a big dictionary, that my grandfather had made as a wedding present for his bride. Into it, I put things that were private to me: letters, my children's baby teeth, my high school boyfriend's class ring, the orchid I wore on my wedding day, and . . . other things that would no longer be private if I told you about them. Next, I established three email accounts: one for work, one for my website, and one personal account that no one else, not even my husband, knows the password to.

Over the years, I have continued to find new ways to honor my privacy, even establishing a "disappearing day"— one day a month when I slip away from my nine (truly!) kids, my husband, and my 2.5 full-time jobs. On this day, I turn off my phone and I am, barring a true emergency, the sole proprietor of my time. You'd be surprised how few true emergencies there are. When I come back home after my blissful eight hours away, I swear I look three years younger.

Last, and probably least important (because it's tangible), I keep the proverbial cash stash that every wise woman I've ever known has kept—whether to provide something one of her children needs or to give herself the occasional bliss moment, however small, of retail therapy. Over the years, my "me-money" has paid for such little luxuries as a writing getaway in a cabin with no phone and, yes, the occasional shot of Botox. But the best thing I ever bought with it was a tiny ruby on a chain for my son to give his first true love when she moved to Australia.

The privacy requirement passed by osmosis to my children much earlier than I got the message. Of course, I still pry into their lives, and they into mine. But I rarely invade. One day, I heard my teenage daughter Francie complaining to a friend about how her conversations with me "make me want to set myself on fire." The friend commiserated: "Mothers!" she said. "They search your drawers, hack into your Facebook, and eavesdrop on your conversations!"

Francie gasped. "My mom's crazy, but she would never do that!"

How much higher are the privacy stakes for young women

today! Back in the day, I made tipsy, desperate late-night calls, but they couldn't be blasted around the world in eighty seconds (accompanied by a regrettable photo). And this is why I am telling you, Dear Reader, that a sense of privacy is the best gift I ever gave myself. My box of trifles, my private email address, and my "disappearing day" are small things. What they form is huge. It's an invisible moat. It doesn't isolate me; it protects me. And it will protect you, too.

**JACQUELYN MITCHARD'S** first novel, *The Deep End of the Ocean*, was Oprah's first-ever Book Club selection and was named by *USA Today* as one of the ten most influential books of the past twenty-five years—second only to the Harry Potter series. Her latest novel is *Second Nature: A Love Story*. Mitchard is fifty-five.

# What 30 means to me

## BY RACHEL ROY

### DISCOVERING JUST HOW STRONG
### I REALLY AM

In my early twenties, I wasn't the girl I am now. I had no idea what I was capable of. It was a challenging time: I was the mother of a young daughter, Ava, and I knew I was going to get a divorce. Of course, that was painful, but I had had time to settle it in my heart, and now I was moving forward, throwing myself into being a mom and starting my own clothing company.

Because I've always tried to give my daughter my best, I decided to give her a sibling. I wanted her to be able to look into the eyes of someone who had the exact same experience as her. My soon-to-be-ex-husband agreed, so we had a second daughter together, Tallulah. Meanwhile, my company was fighting to survive. Factories did not want to produce my collection, and every two weeks, I had to figure out how I was going to pay my employees.

But I persevered, not because I was ambitious—I have never felt that word described me—but because I loved design, I loved fashion. I loved the drama and scale of it. I drew strength from that passion, worked diligently, and slowly my commitment began to pay off. The first big break I got was when I was about thirty-one. A buyer for Bergdorf Goodman saw a beaded camisole I'd made and took my collection without any questions. Her confidence in me pushed me to create better designs, to really get it right—not only for myself but for her, because she put her name on the line for me.

But as grateful as I am to everyone who's ever believed in me, and to all of the kind, generous, hardworking women who have advised me and inspired me, I've learned in my thirties that we have to make our own success. Hard work and loving what you do create the only path to greatness. There's no cheating life. I don't care if you're rich; I don't care if you have connections; I don't care if you're beautiful. You can't rely on others to carry you where you want to go. Build your own path, follow your own dreams, and—I promise—you *will* discover how powerful you truly are.

---

**RACHEL ROY**, thirty-eight, designs the fashion collections Rachel Roy New York and Rachel Rachel Roy. She was inducted into the Council of Fashion Designers of America (CFDA) in 2007.

9

A résumé that is not even
the slightest bit padded.

## BY JULIE ROTTENBERG
## AND ELISA ZURITSKY

By thirty, you want to have accomplished something *real* in the work world. Making your mark professionally is, after all, an important part of becoming an adult. And if you feel you haven't quite made it to where you imagined you'd be at thirty, it can be tempting to fudge your résumé *juuuuust* a little. Don't! By embellishing your accomplishments, you're only selling yourself short. Instead of giving yourself a *fair* chance to make that mark, you risk embarrassing yourself, losing the job, and possibly winding up in a scene like this:

INT. A SWANK, MODERN OFFICE where KIM, the
applicant, sits across from SIMONE, a scary
executive, who reviews Kim's résumé.

SIMONE:

So, Columbia College, class of '05.
My alma mater.


KIM:

Roar, Lions, roar!


SIMONE:

Oh, and I see you were at Zinc
Design for a while. Tell me what an
"associate coordinator of digital
strategy" does . . . ?


KIM:

Oh, well, I worked on the site
relaunch and acted as liaison
between David and our tech vendors.


SIMONE:

Yes, I can read what's here. But
what specifically did you
contribute? (pause) Were you
vetting the wireframes for the
projects? Did you write code for
him? Talk to the developers,
architects . . . what?


*By 30, you should have . . .*

KIM:

Um, I was more involved in the
preproduction stages, managing
communications, gathering the
necessary data, compiling it,
organizing it . . .

SIMONE:

So you were an administrative
assistant.

KIM
(upbeat):
That's another way of saying it,
yes.

SIMONE
(makes a notation on the résumé):
And it says here you're experienced
with content management systems?

KIM:

Mmm-hmm.

SIMONE:

So what back-end platforms have you
worked with?

KIM:

Ummm, wow, let's see . . .

There's a long pause while Kim thinks. And
sweats.

SIMONE:

Well, let's say you had a choice of
using one CMS or another. What
platform would you be most
comfortable with?

KIM:

Well—I mean, it's all changing so
fast, I'd need a little refreshing.

SIMONE:

Okay, so then let's switch gears.
What forms of social media are you
fluent in right now?

KIM:

Facebook.

SIMONE
(turning to her computer):
Oh, good, so show me how Zinc Design
uses Facebook to bring in new
business. We've got a big Facebook

*By 30, you should have . . .*

app in the works, maybe that's
something you could jump into?

KIM:

Well, actually, what I meant was I
have a Facebook page and over two
thousand friends. So I'm on a lot.
Oh, and I have a lot of followers
on Twitter.

SIMONE
(sighs):

It also says here you were an
associate producer for Jimmy
Louden—is that *the* Jimmy Louden,
the film and theater producer?

KIM:

Yes, ma'am. That was intense. Crazy
hours. But great. He's really a
mentor to me.

SIMONE:

Okay. And what aspect of production
were you involved in?

KIM:

Well, I took care of his personal
productions, his pet projects. I was
at his apartment first thing in the

```
morning, last thing at night, and a
few times during the day. Let's just
say I cleaned up a lot of messes.

              SIMONE:
You were his dog walker, weren't
you?

Kim's face says it all.

              SIMONE:
I think we're done here.
```

Of course, we know one *can* glean a lot from the dog walker's vantage point, or the temp's, or even the housekeeper's, so why overstate it? When you tell the humble truth, you also give yourself the opportunity to explain from the heart why you're committed to moving beyond where you are right now to do the wonderful things you're capable of. So stick to your real life story; when you think about it, you've probably accomplished a lot, and if there are dreams you haven't hit yet? Don't fudge 'em. Just start.

---

**JULIE ROTTENBERG AND ELISA ZURITSKY**, both forty-two, were three-time Emmy- and Writers Guild–nominated writers and producers for HBO's *Sex and the City*. Their personal essays and humor pieces have appeared in *The New York Times*, *Slate*, and *Glamour*. They are currently writers and co-executive producers on NBC's *Smash*.

| *By 30, you should have . . .*

One friend who always makes you laugh and one who lets you cry.

## BY KELLY CORRIGAN

You never know until you know, you know? You hope your friends are what you think they are—loyal, deep, fast—but you don't find out for sure until, say, a big lump in your breast turns out to be a bad tumor. Shannon called from vacation in tears when she heard my news. Mellie hired me a housecleaner. Carolann knitted me a warm, kicky beret that I wore for months, until it began to fall apart and my husband said I looked like a forty-year-old pothead. One by one, in choreographed succession, Phoebe, Tracy, and Missy packed bags and came from points east to California, because they "had to be with me." They didn't know what they were doing—my cancer was a first for all of us—but they came anyway. They brought things—art supplies for my two kids, books for my husband, slippers and sleeping caps for me.

And all this came as quite a surprise to me. Had I earned *this much* support?

I had lived most of my life in the company of men. When I was growing up, my older brothers dominated our house, as much with their giant bags of sweaty ice hockey equipment that filled the laundry room as with their epic tales of triumph at the boy-girl dance. I lived in the space that was left over, sometimes boldly (if ineffectively) inserting myself into the action but mostly saving my voice for a later day. I've often pretended that I preferred hanging out with men. After all, I had learned how to cuss like a sea hand and tell a joke like a bartender, and damn it, I wasn't going to rein myself in for a bunch of lily-livered "ladies" who bored me with their small talk about wrap dresses and Pilates and sisal rugs.

But it was the ladies who saved me, physically and emotionally. My surgeon was a woman, as were my ob-gyn, my chemo nurse, my radiation oncologist, my genetic counselor, and the psychologist who gave us the words "cancer is like weeds in a garden," a phrase my husband and I used over and over again with our small children (who are, incidentally, both girls). When my fertility was sacrificed to the cause, I found the empathy I so needed in the arms of Mary, Hope, and then Meg and then my mother, all of whom knew to listen for a long time (days) before reminding me that the two girls I already had were double-good and would surely fill me up if I let them. Maybe it was the central role my breasts were suddenly playing in things, but looking back, it was a distinctly feminine time and one that left me wiser than it found me.

Since then, since I've become a regular person again instead of a cancer patient, I've kept a soft spot in my heart for guy friends, but I woo girlfriends. I cultivate and collect them because I know. Believe me, I *know*.

**KELLY CORRIGAN**, forty-four, is the author of *The Middle Place* and *Lift*. She is a YouTube sensation whose beloved "Transcending" video was sent woman-to-woman to more than 4 million viewers. She is the founder of circusofcancer.org.

A set of screwdrivers, a cordless drill,

and a black lace bra.

Something ridiculously expensive that
you bought for yourself, just because
you deserve it.

## BY THE EDITORS OF *GLAMOUR*

NOW, WAIT, WAIT. WE'RE NOT SUGGESTING THAT YOU
buy anything you can't afford. In fact, denying your "wants"
some of the time is a very smart thing (see number seven on
this list, Suze Orman's passionate plea that you save money).
You may *want* that luxury handbag, but you *need* a retirement
fund more, and you're wise not to shell out cash impulsively
each time the feeling strikes. But even Suze would agree: One
of the greatest payoffs of having your financial life in order
is to be able to spend that money on *yourself* once in a while.

But not all of us do. We ache to see Paris for the first
time—but can't shake the notion that a guy should take us
there. We stalk the same diamond studs on the Tiffany website for over a year—but again, shouldn't those be a gift? We
even squirrel away enough cash to buy, drumroll, *our own
place*. But we just . . . can't . . . seem . . . to pull the trigger.

And why is that? If you've never spoiled yourself because

to do so would mean going into debt, then a wise woman are you. But if the reason you haven't done whatever it takes to afford your dream trip or, heck, your dream custom surfboard is that you're listening to the inner voice that tells you . . .

> *You're too greedy,*
> *You're too young,*
> *You're too single,*
> *Those things are for real grown-ups,*
> *Someone else will buy them for you,* or
> *You don't deserve them anyway . . .*

. . . then (we mean this in the nicest possible way): Get over it!

Saving up to buy things you want and deserve is a way of taking control of your life and your happiness, of recognizing that no one but you is responsible for getting you what you want in this world. It also says to everyone around you: "I treat myself well—so *you* should treat me that way too." The first step, of course, is building your savings account. But once you've got some fallback money in the bank, let yourself have something you love from time to time. After all, why should you wait for a knight in shining armor to give you a ride when you can afford to buy the horse yourself? If you hold out too long, you just might miss the sunset.

## 13

The *belief* that you deserve it.

### BY FIONA MAAZEL

YOU DESERVE GREATNESS—NOW GO FOR IT. THAT'S just the kind of sentiment my mom spent years trying to impress upon me. The way she'd put it: Shoot for the lamppost and you might hit the hydrant; shoot for the moon and you might hit the lamppost. She'd say this over dinner and I'd roll my eyes, even though she'd accomplished a lot (three separate careers, in fact) with this attitude. "How else to get there unless you believe?" she'd ask. "That's what it takes to be a successful woman." It took me about thirty years to listen.

Throughout my teens and most of my twenties, I had the idea I was dim, unaccomplished, and just not worth anyone's time. Perhaps this was because my mom *was* successful, as was my dad, and my older brother was an obvious talent at pretty much everything he did. I suppose I knew other girls who also felt inferior to everyone else, though we didn't talk about it. What was there to say? Most of us had been well loved and brought up to believe in ourselves, and yet we didn't.

Even so, by the time I was twenty-two, I had many of the things that make a life look good from the outside. I'd gone to a good school, I had friends, I was reasonably attractive, and I was working at a magazine most people esteemed highly. But if you asked me to reason through why I had all these blessings in my life, I'd have called it luck. Or I'd have said nothing. I just couldn't see that the good in my life was my doing. And in this, you'll find the essence of low self-esteem: It doesn't answer to reason. It doesn't answer to anything.

So I worked at this literary magazine. I had latent pretensions about wanting to be a writer, but, come on, only *really* smart people got to be writers. I bartended at night—this awful bar called Prowl, whose best patron used to write me vampire poetry on cocktail napkins—and I met guys there whose money not even a prostitute would take. But I went out with them anyway. I dated Gary, who moved in with me for two weeks, then rode off on his motorcycle without a word. I dated Matt, who once starred in a pornographic movie but left me to become a rabbi. I thought at length about writing these stories down—about writing anything down—but I didn't. Who cared about the experiences, thoughts, and feelings of a girl who'd accomplished so little? Forget shooting for the moon—I couldn't even shoot for the trash.

But then I was twenty-five and wanted to write a piece about women's wrestling. I'd stumbled on a clip of these women in leotards flexing in a ring and thought: *There are women who can do this? Who? Why?* I flew out to San Diego for a convention, and there I met some women who blew me away. Big women. Women with large hair in bikinis who marched around the ring like they owned it. Like they owned the world. I asked one of the wrestlers where she got her confidence, and she said, "Honey, if you want what we have, hang out with us and find out."

In some ways, I did hang out awhile. I left the convention but tried to stay in the head space of the women I'd met there. I walked a little taller. And started seeing a lamppost here and there.

I pitched the wrestling article to a glossy magazine, and it was a go. To be honest, the article wasn't very good, and the magazine never paid me, even though they published it. Life is not a fairy tale; it's a parade of events that help you accrue wisdom and courage and faith. You learn first that you *can* and, later, that you *should*. I framed the article. And I thought vaguely about suing the magazine because I'd worked hard and deserved to get paid, and frankly, I deserved to get paid much more than they had offered. And when lightning didn't strike me down for thinking that either, maybe I started looking up at the night sky with some ideas in mind.

I was still making spreadsheets at the fancy literary magazine, but with a new sense that maybe I could be doing something more. And then something happened that popped the strutting writer in me out into the world. I spent my twenty-fifth birthday in the hospital. I had pancreatitis. I couldn't do anything and I did not care. Halfway through my ten-day stay, a woman came in with toxic shock syndrome, which blossomed into something incurable and terrifying. Her agony made mine feel like a chipped tooth. Apparently, she'd gotten sick thanks to self-neglect and a drinking problem. Her family came to visit one day; on their way out, one of them shook his head and muttered, "If you want what she has, hang out in her world."

After that, I started to write more. As much as possible, all of the time. I didn't want what that poor woman had. I didn't want to be in that place of self-doubt and low-esteem where the rest of life was forbidden to me. I wanted the opposite. I wanted to walk through life like I owned it. I wasn't going to change overnight, but I was committed, this time, to thinking differently about myself. If I went out with a guy and he was anything less than gentlemanly: the boot! If I got work, I made sure I was paid for it. If I wrote a sentence, I kept it. I kept them all. And so I wrote a ton. My fiction wasn't very good, but if everyone else deserved to be writing, so did I.

One day I decided to submit a short story (under a pseudonym) to the esteemed magazine at which I worked. Didn't I deserve to be in the pantheon of my heroes? Actually, no. The staff slaughtered my writing. Most of them guessed I was the author and did not try hard to pretend otherwise. They gave me looks. I'm sure they laughed when I left the room.

But still: I was proud of myself. The old me would have plummeted into a hole of self-loathing so deep it would've taken me months to crawl out. But the new me said: Okay, that didn't go so well. Guess I have to work harder. Lesson learned. I'd aimed for the moon. And I've been aiming ever since.

**FIONA MAAZEL**, thirty-seven, is the author of the novel *Last Last Chance*. She is a National Book Foundation "5 Under 35" honoree, recipient of a Lannan Residency Fellowship, and winner of the Bard Prize for Fiction in 2009. Her new novel, *Woke Up Lonely*, is forthcoming.

# *What 30 means to me*

## BY PADMA LAKSHMI

### BEING GRATEFUL FOR LIFE'S GIFTS

At thirty-six, after years of living with severe, sometimes debilitating menstrual pain, I was finally diagnosed with endometriosis—a disorder in which uterine tissue grows outside the uterus, becoming trapped in the body. I was told my case was so severe I'd never be able to have a child naturally. It was heartbreaking. As my doctor was preparing me for much-needed surgery, he said, "Don't worry, we're going to go in laparoscopically, so the scars will be really small. I'm very sensitive to minimizing them for women because I know how it is."

I said, "Oh, no, I'm grateful for my scars."

But that hasn't always been the case.

I was in a terrible car accident as a teenager. I was fourteen years old and on my way back with my parents from a

Hindu temple in Malibu. We flew off the freeway and forty feet down an embankment. We hit a tree dead-on—it stopped our fall before crashing into the roof. When they tore the car open with the Jaws of Life and found us, my arm was across my mother's chest and had taken most of the impact of the tree. She still broke five ribs and her sternum and had a cardiac contusion, but she survived.

Amazingly, we all did. I fractured my hip, and my arm was operated on. I healed well but was left with a long scar. It was half an inch wide and seven inches long.

When I first got that scar, I was self-conscious about it. I perfected a casual pose that hid it under my left hand and thumb when my arms were crossed. I saw it as something to be embarrassed about and wore long white gloves to the prom. When I became a model, I got even better at camouflaging it, with long sleeves, makeup, and chemical dermabrasion. Then a miraculous thing happened. I was called for a photo shoot with the great photographer Helmut Newton. When I arrived, I found that one of my closest friends had been booked as the makeup artist. When he saw that I had nearly eradicated the scar with dermabrasion, he gasped, "What have you done? Why have you erased part of it? You've ruined its beauty!" And he set to work touching up the scar, adding wine-colored lipstick to the lightened areas.

After that, I began to feel differently about my scar. It was a symbol of my survival, after all, and my mother's, too. As I evolved into my thirties, I even became thankful for it—this reminder that life is unpredictable and fragile. It has taught me so much about perspective: When times get tough, I always try to say, "It could have been worse."

By thirty, I believe we should all focus more on feeling gratitude for the gifts we've been given. The more grateful we feel for our families, for our friends, for the good health we have, the more we will nourish those things for the future. And that also goes for the parts of our bodies that aren't improving with age, the parts we want not to like. I always say, "What gravity took away from me, I hope I have gained in gravitas."

And so I give thanks to all the scars on my body. They form the map of my life: I can tell a story about every imprint on my skin. There are the mosquito bites on my back from when I slept under the Sardinian sun the summer I first fell in love; the scrapes on my leg from the rocks in the Cuban sea during the filming of my first movie; the tiny line near my belly button from my endometriosis surgery; and most of all, the C-section scar that wouldn't exist if I'd never gotten the scar that came before it.

Today, I am a mother and the cofounder of an organization that helps young women with endometriosis. These are the roles I'm most proud of as a woman. Of course, no one can be proud of *everything*. But by the time we're in our thirties, I believe we should strive to own and respect who we are, regardless of our struggles and difficulties. After all, even every little and big mistake, like every scar, can be a lesson in humility—one of the greatest gifts of all.

**PADMA LAKSHMI**, forty-one, is the host of Bravo's *Top Chef* and author of the cookbooks *Easy Exotic* and *Tangy Tart Hot & Sweet*.

**14** A skin-care regimen, an exercise routine, and a plan for dealing with those few other facets of life that don't get better after 30.

## BY ANGIE HARMON

I WAS ANXIOUS ABOUT TURNING THIRTY SIMPLY BE-cause I had heard that I should be—you hear it all your life. After a while you start to get the feeling that they're not going to roll out a birthday cake on your thirtieth birthday; they're going to roll out a coffin.

In your twenties, it's easy to have a sense of immortality because you look amazing no matter what you do. You can have a lot to drink and be hungover and peek in the mirror and still think, *Wow, I don't look half as bad as I feel.* But in your thirties, you *look* hungover when you're hungover. You *look* tired when you're tired.

I'm not gonna lie: I was scared.

But I have good news from the other side! Your face will not fall off. You'll look exactly the same on the first day of your thirties as you do on the last night of your twenties. And while your twenties are fun, it's in your thirties that you become more aware of your body and more familiar with it. You own it. It's an empowerment and a transformation. With age comes respect.

Part of that respect is knowing how to take care of yourself. You get only one body in this lifetime, and you have to be good to it. And so I offer you ten tricks for looking fierce at any age, especially the one you are now:

1. Eat foods that are good for you. Your outsides are a reflection of what you're putting into your insides. Those French fries will catch up to you—that's a fact.

2. Make friends with the elliptical machine. It's cardio that works everything in one shot—your arms, your butt, and your legs. What will you do with all your extra time?

3. Buy swimsuits that *fit*. One-pieces can be sexy, too.

4. You need to exfoliate for young-looking skin. End of discussion.

5. Never underestimate the power of a bright lipstick. Try a hydrating one with anti-aging ingredients.

6. Sun protection is a must, always, even if you're no longer lounging all day by the beach in a skimpy bikini. Even if you're walking, driving, flying. Protect your skin with SPF.

7. Let your moisturizer sink in for three minutes before putting makeup or other products on.

8. Reconsider your beauty routine. Your hair and skin texture and color can change over time—so should the products you use.

9. Know that there's always going to be something about your body you're not going to like. (I would love for my bottom to do what it's supposed to do, but it doesn't.) We *all* have imperfections. Accept them—they make us unique and wonderful.

10. That said, there will be times when self-acceptance comes less easily. And for those days, there is *always* going to be something you can wear to make yourself feel better. Thank you, Spanx!

**ANGIE HARMON**, thirty-nine, is a film and television actress currently starring on the TNT drama *Rizzoli & Isles*. She began her career as an international runway and print model; in 2001 she married NFL star Jason Sehorn, with whom she has three daughters.

A solid start on a satisfying career, a satisfying relationship, and all those other facets of life that *do* get better.

## BY KATIE COURIC

I SPENT MY TWENTIES FOCUSING ON MY CAREER— first as a desk assistant at ABC News, an assignment editor at CNN, then as a local reporter in Miami and Washington. My work certainly took precedence over my love life. Yes, I dated a lot and it was fun, but I wasn't ready to fully commit myself to another person. It was my selfish decade. I wanted to be a network correspondent by the time I was thirty, and I thought it would be easier to climb the career ladder if I had flexibility and independence.

While I didn't quite make my deadline by age thirty, the hard work paid off when I was thirty-two. That's when the legendary Tim Russert from NBC News called and asked me to come to his office. He said he had been watching me and was impressed by my work—I wasn't the most glamorous reporter, but I was probably one of the scrappiest. Then he said, "I'd like to hire you to be our deputy Pentagon correspondent."

It was such a thrill. I think that's when I thought, *Wow. I'm on my way.*

Two years later, when the folks at NBC asked me to be a substitute anchor on the *Today* show, I thought they were crazy. I had always been a reporter first and foremost and had never even used a teleprompter. My first morning reading the news, I was a nervous wreck. I remember talking at the end of my first newscast about a guy who had been lost skiing and was found after lighting his cash on fire. I threw back to Bryant Gumbel and Deborah Norville, saying something like "With my luck, I would have only had change." And they laughed! I suddenly realized I might have a future here.

As I began to meet my professional goals, I had an epiphany: I didn't want just a career. I didn't want to be that girl who says, "Oh my God, I can't believe I forgot to have children!" So I became more receptive to meeting people. That's when I found my husband, who was everything I wanted in a partner.

Just as I'd planned *everything* in my twenties, *nothing* went according to plan for the next decade of my life. Like my two pregnancies, for example. I was offered a full-time co-anchor position on the *Today* show by an executive who didn't know I was pregnant. When I told him I was, he said, "Well, you have really lousy timing." My response: "Does this mean you're not going to be knitting me baby booties anytime soon?"

But for me, having children after thirty was great. I had that solid start on my career, so I didn't worry too much about choosing between motherhood and professional success. I was ready to have them both.

Of course, not every surprise the universe throws at you is a happy one. The next unexpected event in our lives was my husband's cancer. Losing him was devastating, but my girls and I got through it together. They are the two best things that ever happened to me, and I feel so, so lucky to have them.

The ability to accept and adapt gracefully to life's twists and turns is one of the greatest skills you'll learn. Should you plan for the things you want? Absolutely. But if you're not exactly where you wanted to be, exactly when you wanted to be there, don't sweat it. I hadn't met the career goals I'd hoped to reach by thirty, but I got there eventually, and made time for love, too. *That's* what matters.

**KATIE COURIC**, fifty-five, former *CBS Evening News* anchor and *Today* show host, is making a return to daytime TV with her own talk show on ABC. The award-winning journalist also writes books and is a former columnist for *Glamour.*

By 30, you

should know…

# 1

How to fall in love without losing yourself.

## BY MELISSA DE LA CRUZ

WHAT YOU ARE ABOUT TO READ IS A FABLE, THOUGH it's inspired by the all-too-true experiences of many women we know. It's a cautionary tale about a girl named Jess who had a way of losing herself every time she fell in love. Love, of course, is a wonderful thing, a grand adventure of the heart. But while it's thrilling to get caught up in its wake, don't forget to hold on to who you are—or that incredible person might get swept away. That's what happened to Jess.

Like many young women in their twenties, Jess wanted a lot in life: a bigger apartment, a promotion, new ankle booties, and a loving boyfriend. She was a meticulous dresser, kept her sunny studio apartment spotlessly clean, and loved her job. She was curious about the city she lived in and drawn to the many things it offered, like art museums; tiny, interesting restaurants; awe-inspiring concerts; and even, when she was feeling ambitious, the occasional Shakespeare production. She had a great sense of humor and many friends. She was always busy on weekend nights. Jess was a go-getter. She had a good head on her shoulders. And she was in love with love.

When Jess fell in love, she *fell* in love: headfirst, eyes wide shut, throwing herself into the relationship with her entire body and soul. So much so that every time it happened, she would become a whole new person.

She met Baseball Billy at her corner bar one evening and was immediately smitten with his crooked grin and muscular arms—even though sports bored her to tears and she would have rather spent her Friday nights listening to a violin quartet than doing the seventh-inning stretch. She stopped eating at her favorite French-Vietnamese place because Billy ate at only "chain" restaurants (to match the one he wore around his neck, she liked to joke).

But Jess's relationship with Billy stopped being a source of amusement to her friends when she started canceling plans, ignoring book club, and giving away theater tickets to be with him. They began to complain: What the hell? When would they see Jess? But the two stopped dating a few months later, and Jess was heartbroken, especially since she'd spent her entire year's shoe budget on tickets to the World Series, which she had no interest in seeing. Thankfully, there was always eBay. Problem solved, and new platforms to boot. (Jess liked puns.)

But when she met Sci-Fi Sam, Jess decided to try even harder. She fell in love with his quirky sense of humor and owlish glasses. It was a relief to be with someone whose vocabulary wasn't limited to "Babe" and "Get me a beer, would ya, hon?" She read every one of Sam's far-fetched science-fiction screenplays and learned how to say "I love you" in Klingon without giggling. On Halloween, she dressed up as Uhura to his Captain Kirk; she fought through the crowds in her uncomfortable Amidala headdress at Comic-Con; and she watched every episode of *Stargate* and *Torchwood* on Friday nights with the same intense devotion she used to give to *Mad Men*.

More than anything, though, Jess wanted a relationship to last. She was obsessed with finding The One, and although she was only twenty-nine, she began to have an irrational fear that her city was filling up with smarter, younger, prettier girls every day who would take her right out of the running. She had to put a ring on it. It was time to get serious.

The next two years were a parade of boys—and the worlds that went with them. There was Alt-Rock Andy (suddenly her iPod was filled with bands she'd never heard of, whose song lyrics she mauled when she sang along); next, Hockey Hal (now Fridays were at Madison Square Garden, and Jess discovered there was a certain thrill to pounding the glass and yelling); then Pretentious Pete (an aspiring writer whose short stories she could not understand but pretended to love); and finally, Hipster Harry (for him, she cut her hair into choppy layers to look more like the girls at the clubs they partied in till dawn).

She'd given everything to every boy she'd ever fallen in love with, and after a dizzying and devastating run of it, Jess woke up one day in Harry's drafty loft and looked in the mirror: "Who am I?" she asked, appalled to see a girl with messy hair and tired eyes, wearing a baseball cap and a flannel button-down over a World of Warcraft T-shirt, along with skinny jeans that were *so* unflattering on her. What had happened?

But instead of despairing, Jess laughed out loud. One thing she'd never misplaced was her sense of humor. Seeing her reflection, she remembered: "I am Jessica. I like J.Crew cardigans and extra-large Frappuccinos and fresh flowers and clean apartments and real dates with men who care about who *I* am. I'm going to call my friends and start paying attention to my work. I will comb my hair, I will renew my theater subscription, I will go see the new Picasso exhibit. And I will never, ever again pretend to love video games." She breathed a deep, stress-melting sigh. Getting to know Jess again was going to be the coolest thing she'd done in a long, long time. And the rest, she was suddenly certain, would all fall into place.

Which, of course, it did.

---

**MELISSA DE LA CRUZ**, forty, is the author of the Blue Bloods series for teens. Her books for adults include *Witches of East End* and *Serpent's Kiss*.

How you feel about having kids.

**BY RACHEL ZOE**

SEE, I ALWAYS KNEW I WANTED TO BE A MOM. I'M A very maternal person—I love to take care of people, I love to problem-solve, I'm always worried about everybody else. So in one way I've been lucky, because I've had my feelings all figured out. I wasn't sure how I would make motherhood work with my career, but I knew I wanted to make it happen. And that's something women have to know, deep down, as they get older. Would you regret not having kids? Because after you hit thirty, the ticking clock kicks in—and whether you like it or not, Mother Nature forces you to make some decisions.

My husband, Rodger, and I are both kind of like grown-up kids ourselves. We have a very career-driven, jet-set life-style, and in the past I've had to be selfish in dedicating all my time and energy to my work as a stylist. Because I always knew what having kids involved, I didn't want to commit to it if I couldn't be present and hands-on. After a while, though, I started to feel like I might never get there.

Then, when I was thirty-eight, I realized a whole decade had gone by since I'd started to seriously consider motherhood. Rodger and I had already been together twenty years, and we were running out of time. So we decided, "Hey, let's wing it. Let's just see what happens." And the first time out of the gate, I got pregnant! Everyone had me convinced that because I was older, it would take me two years of trying and fertility treatments and all that. But we were very lucky.

Our son, Skyler, is so amazing. The whole thing's just been unbelievable. I mean, labor's not fun; I'll tell you that. If anyone says it is, they're lying. But I couldn't be happier with our decision to bring a baby into our lives. I do have two full-time jobs now, and it's definitely hard because all I want to do is be with my baby at the end of the day. But if you want it all badly enough, you figure out how to make it work.

For some women, the career is enough—having kids doesn't feel right, and I totally get that. But if you *do* want to have kids at some point, I have two pieces of advice. The first is: Don't wait! I missed the window of being a young mom, and I'm super envious of my friends who had kids earlier than I did, because they can take their time and choose to have another child (or several!) if they want.

The second: Remember that there are many paths to motherhood. What's right for you might be adopting, or finding a surrogate, or maybe your version of motherhood is just being the best aunt ever. The point is that the path is in your hands.

And once you get there? Believe me: It's love on a whole other level.

**RACHEL ZOE**, forty, is a Hollywood stylist and the star of Bravo's hit reality show *The Rachel Zoe Project*. She recently launched her own clothing line, the Rachel Zoe Collection.

and confront a friend without ruining the friendship.

When to try harder and when
to walk away.

**BY KATHY GRIFFIN**

I've never had a hard time with "when to try harder"—that would be every day. The "when to walk away" piece of it has been harder for me to learn.

I've got a strong work ethic, which comes from my parents—they put in very hard, very long hours to support their five kids. And when I first started working as a stand-up comic, I looked around and got the picture real fast: If you're a female in a male-driven business, you'd better not stop even for a second. Since day one as a comic, I've had to try harder than my male counterparts to keep myself out there, and by age thirty, I was in total shark mode: moving forward, moving forward, moving forward.

I've been told "no" way more than I've been told "yes" in my career, but it just makes me want to work harder and jump higher. I'm the cockroach that's going to be here after the apocalypse. My comedy has gotten me banned from more TV shows than I can count, but the one thing no one can ever stop me from doing is stand-up. So if I'm banned from every network in the world, I will still tour. I think a very key thing for women is to refuse to let anyone tell you you're banned, you're out of fashion, you don't look the right way. Put your energy into a career that will be there for you regardless of the naysayers.

Of course, I don't treat my romantic relationships like that, because that would make me a crazy stalker. You *should* walk away from a relationship when it's not good for you anymore. I didn't always know this. I used to believe it was justifiable to do anything to find and keep a guy—throw yourself at him, try to convince him to like you. To be honest, I'm still confused about relationships. Heterosexual men are like Martians to me—they may as well have antennae and arrive on a spaceship instead of picking me up in a Prius. I will spend the rest of my life trying to understand them. But I *have* learned that love is the one area where women should give themselves a break and cut bait. Men are better at that—if a guy isn't feeling great about the relationship, he will leave and not look back. As women, we're more analytical and more accommodating. We tend to hang in there and try harder. But if you're with a dude who's texting other girls, bye-bye. That's an important lesson to learn.

Overall, though, enjoy perseverance. It gets a bad rap, but I consider it a great compliment when people tell me I'm a hard worker. Are my motivations completely pure? No way.

A lot of my drive has to do with getting back at the mean girls or achieving more than the people who tried to keep me down. But you know what? Those things can be motivators in a healthy way. I've taken being pissed off and turned it into a career.

KATHY GRIFFIN, fifty-one, is a stand-up comedian and star of Bravo's *Kathy Griffin: My Life on the D-List*, for which she's won two Emmys. She's also a Grammy nominee and the author of the memoir *Official Book Club Selection*.

5 | How to kiss in a way that communicates perfectly what you would and wouldn't like to happen next.

**BY THE EDITORS OF *GLAMOUR***

Every kiss has its own meaning. As the early-twentieth-century French chanteuse Mistinguett said: "A kiss can be a comma, a question mark, or an exclamation point. That's basic spelling that every woman ought to know." So what would *you* like to spell? Well, let's run down some possibilities:

If your point is *No need to be so nervous, Mr. Second Date, I like you already!* try this: Lean in confidently, touch his shoulder or hair and quiet his lips with a playful peck. Pull away, smile, and watch him melt with happy relief.

If you want to let an overeager (but appealing) guy know *This is a kiss but* just *a kiss. You're sleeping alone tonight*: Take his hand and twine your fingers in his as you kiss. It's a surprisingly sexy way to remind him you're keeping track of that hand. And if things still get hotter and heavier than you'd like, a gentle squeeze signals, Slow down.

If he's overeager and *un*appealing, you can always slap him. But if he doesn't quite deserve that, there *is* a kind and graceful way to say *Please stop*: Just place your palm on his chest and exert a pressure slightly greater than the force of his kiss. (Plan B: Push *hard*.)

If you're ready to convey—if not outright say—*I want you* to him: Well, few things are more telling of one's state of heart than the hypercharged moment *before* a kiss. Lock eyes, look deeply, and tilt your head slightly before letting your gaze travel to his lips and back again; then, when you can hardly bear it a second longer, close those baby browns and . . . yes, he'll hear you.

But a great communicator *listens* as well as speaks. "Terrific kissers are like bamboo," said one guy we consulted on the subject. Say what? "You have to bend but not break," he explained. "Bad kissers think too hard, plan *too* much. Good kissers are flexible. They try things out with you." Another man we consulted (an award-winning novelist known for his steamy love scenes) summed it up like this: "Men might sometimes seem to take kissing for granted, to focus only on what *we* hope is coming next. But remind us how erotic a kiss can be: It really is an understanding two people can reach without words." And we all need that.

# What 30 means to me

## BY SANDRA LEE

### IT'S TIME TO JUST GO FOR IT!

The day you turn thirty is a big deal; it's when you're really starting to come into your own. If you were a rose, you would be just starting to open up and show all your layers of petals.

So if you're melancholy about hitting this milestone (like I was, for about two days), here's what I say to you: Take a moment or the whole day and do what you love. Listen to your favorite music, loudly. Go for a nice long walk in your favorite park, or punch your favorite punching bag, even if that's your pillow. Do whatever you need to do to own the day and start considering what the rest of your life could be. How many petals do you want to have on your rose? You can have as many as your heart desires.

I wanted a lot of petals. I wanted a full, lush life. That's one thing I've known since I was a little girl, living on welfare and food stamps. I was never focused on finding the right guy. I focused on building a life full of meaning and possibility, grounded in simple good values.

In my twenties I launched my first company, Kurtain Kraft, a line of do-it-yourself curtain hardware that was successful beyond my wildest dreams. I sold the line on QVC and traveled the country going to state fairs and home-and-garden shows, talking one-on-one with the consumer. I loved connecting with the women I met. I spoke their language because I came from their world.

But what I'd never had, at thirty, was a real mentor. Someone to show me the ropes and give me the inside scoop. Someone who had been there and done that—who had lived the life lessons I had yet to learn. I had grown up with very little parental input, so I learned to be über-responsible, self-reliant, and self-sufficient. As a result, I never wanted to seem like I needed help or to impose on anyone else. But at thirty, I started thinking, *Wait a minute, there's nothing weak about asking for input and advice.* So I opened the door for myself and received wisdom from some of the strongest, most thoughtful women in my field. I was lucky that these women were kind enough to give me not just a hand up but a real understanding of their knowledge.

In many ways, thanks to their advice and support, I was able to weather the first big storm of my career, an unexpected wave of returns from QVC that flattened my company. But I didn't let it end my career. I dusted off and diversified my knowledge and product line to include gardening, crafts, scrapbooking, and cooking. During this tough time, I found out who my friends really were. If you're successful, you'll have friends who are with you for the moment. They are there because you can afford to be in the room and because you're the big deal of the moment. And when you're *not* the big deal of the moment, you'll look around the room and see the only people who truly care about and support you. These are the important people to remember.

Years ago, one of my real friends, a TV executive and one of my first mentors, Carole, gave me a beautiful little plaque for my birthday. It's inscribed with a famous quote: "What would you attempt to do if you knew you couldn't fail?" When I got that, I thought, *Of course, I would just go for it!* And that's what you've got to do every single day of your thirties and beyond. Just go for it! Your life is now.

---

**SANDRA LEE**, forty-five, is editor-in-chief of *Sandra Lee Semi-Homemade* magazine, the host of two multi-Emmy-nominated cooking shows on Food Network, and the author of twenty-five books. She has been awarded the President's Volunteer Service Award and the Ellis Island Medal of Honor for her contributions to society.

The names of the secretary of state, your great-grandmothers, and the best tailor in town.

GO AHEAD—FILL IN THE BLANKS. WE WON'T JUDGE!

The secretary of state:

_____

Your great-grandmothers:

_____

The best tailor in town:

_____

7

How to live alone,
even if you don't like to.

## BY PAMELA REDMOND SATRAN

WHEN I WAS A KID, THE ONLY WOMAN I KNEW WHO lived alone was my aunt Margie. Although Margie was nice enough in a peppermint-scented, pilly-sweatered kind of way, I figured she lived alone because she had no other choice: She wasn't pretty enough to get a husband or cool enough to have friends or lucky enough to be a mom. Living alone might be better than being dead, I thought, but just barely.

I had no desire to ever live alone myself, and I didn't think I'd ever have to. I moved from my parents' house to a college dorm room, and from my dorm to an apartment with my first husband, and when my teenage marriage broke up, I moved in with a group of friends.

Eventually, though, I found myself too old to keep labeling my cheese but not ready to move in with my adorable but oh-so-tenuous new boyfriend. And so at twenty-three I signed a lease on my first solo apartment. I was thrilled to finally be embarking on a phase that was defined by nothing more than my own moods, schedule, and agenda. But I also dreaded discovering that, alone with my own soul, I'd find nothing very compelling. What if even *I* didn't want to be with me?

It was one of the first pedestrian chores of having my own place that ended up banishing my worry: I had to paint the walls, a job that clearly fell to me alone. But at the same time, I realized, no one else had any right to decide what color I painted those walls, or at what hour, or how I configured the rest of the space around them.

I remember so vividly what a thrill it was to transform the room that I can still see the gorgeous color I chose, the palest shell pink, spreading like a blush of excitement across those walls. There was an important revelation in that moment: Living alone meant pleasing nobody, not even for one second, but myself.

Of course, there were lonely moments too, and those filled with terror: As keenly as I remember the pleasure of blasting "Desperado" for five days running after a painful breakup, I remember how desolate I felt lying alone on the floor crying over him. I recall how horrible I felt upon discovering a mouse swimming desperately in my toilet. (If you must know, I shut my eyes and—yes, shoot me—I flushed.) How terrifying it was to wake up from a nightmare at 3 a.m. and feel there was no one on earth I had a right to call at that hour to comfort me.

There was also a sense that I was doing this until something better—i.e., a permanent man—came along. But while I was waiting, I was also amassing important life skills available only to those who live alone. How to single-handedly haul a dresser up five flights of stairs, say, or how not to eat all the ice cream in your freezer. Where to fortify a door so no one can get in, and when to kick that guy in your bed out.

When it's only you within those pink walls, on the peaceful sunny days as well as the fretful nights, you get to know yourself in a way you don't, you just *can't*, in any other situation. There's no one else to blame the mess on, to absorb the anxiety, to break the silence. You're forced to confront your own weaknesses as well as your strengths, to figure out exactly what you want out of living with a lover or a friend (if you end up wanting that at all), and why being alone may be just perfect.

Due to love or money or some combination of the two, I moved into and out of my own apartments throughout my twenties, finally getting remarried and having my first child in the whirlwind eighteen months before my thirtieth birthday. Except for a week or two when I've been traveling, I haven't lived alone since.

But here's the important thing: I know that I could. I know that—undoubtedly like my aunt Margie—I'd like it. I even know what color I'd paint the walls.

---

**PAMELA REDMOND SATRAN** is the author of the novel *The Possibility of You* and the forthcoming humor book *Rabid*, as well as a creator of the website nameberry.com. A mother of three, she intends to look and act thirty-seven forever.

table or a yoga mat—when your soul needs soothing.

**9**

That you can't change the length
of your legs, the width of your hips,
or the nature of your parents.

## BY PORTIA DE ROSSI

THERE ARE CERTAIN THINGS IN LIFE THAT YOU JUST have to accept—your height, for instance, or the family you're born into. And, yes, the length of your legs or the width of your hips. But the thing is, as women, we are constantly taught the opposite. We're given this message that we can alter every single aspect of our faces and bodies, and we're encouraged to do so to try to achieve this ideal of what a woman is "supposed" to look like. You're expected to *fix* yourself. To dye your hair, or get eyelash extensions, or change the tone of your skin, or the shape of your nose, or the size of your breasts. There is so much *fixing*.

So, as women, we've got to be pretty damn amazing to realize early on that physical perfection is neither achievable nor useful, and that all that fixing can be toxic.

I learned that lesson the hard way myself. From a very early age, I was told that my body was not perfect. I started modeling when I was twelve, and I was scrutinized and looked up and down and told that my hips were too wide, my shoulders too narrow. When I met with my first modeling agency, they told me to go home and call them with my measurements. So I got out a little measuring tape from my mother's sewing kit, measured my bust, waist, and hips, and called them with the numbers. There was a long pause on the other end. Then my new agent said to me, "Let's just say you're 35-25-34. We'll put that on your card."

From that moment on, I thought, *I have to change.* So I spent the entire decade in a state of turmoil and inner torment trying to achieve that perfect body. I ping-ponged from 127 pounds to a shocking 82 pounds to 168 pounds and back down again. But no matter what I did or how much I starved myself, my proportions were the same. My hips were always going to be wider than my shoulders. My legs were always going to be the shape I was born with. If only I had made peace with that by twenty-five, my energy would have been put into much more worthwhile things.

I was thirty when I decided I needed to recover from my eating disorder. I think by the time you're thirty, you've started to get this awareness—at least I had—that you may have been taught the wrong things. I was looking back at how I had lived my twenties, and I realized that what I was doing wasn't working, that I didn't want to live like that for the rest of my life. I knew that there was a better way of living, because I looked at people who weren't obsessed with their bodies like I was, and they seemed a lot happier, calmer, more peaceful. They didn't spend every waking minute thinking of ways to work off every single calorie they ate. They had lives. It was a turning point for me. I had to surrender to the fact that I really wasn't as in control as I'd thought I was. That I'd hit a dead end. I remember thinking, *God, I don't want to be this miserable anymore.*

I'm grateful for the lessons I've learned, but I know I'll never get that decade back—all the time spent weighing myself and not being able to hang out with my friends because I was fixated on changing myself.

You know when you're in yoga and you're looking around, thinking, *Wow, I wish I were that flexible,* or *How come she can hold that pose?* Well, my friend has a saying: "Stay on your own mat." Not physically, but mentally. In life, we're all made differently: our families, our frames, our personalities and talents. Appreciate how you were made, and stay on your mat. *That's* where happiness lies.

---

**PORTIA DE ROSSI**, thirty-nine, is an actress best known for her roles in the TV series *Ally McBeal* and *Arrested Development*. She's also the author of the memoir *Unbearable Lightness: A Story of Loss and Gain*. She lives in Los Angeles with her wife, Ellen DeGeneres.

# 10

That your childhood may not have been perfect, but it's over.

## BY LISA LING

MY CHILDHOOD WAS DEFINITELY NOT PERFECT. MY parents, who are first-generation Chinese, basically had an arranged marriage that should never have been. They fought constantly. I remember trying to make peace, saying, "Mommy, Daddy—kiss!" But it never happened. They got divorced when I was seven years old and my sister, Laura, was four. Right away, our mom moved to Los Angeles to take a job, and Laura and I stayed with our dad in Carmichael, California.

When you're ethnic and your parents divorce, it adds a whole new layer of challenge to your life because you already feel like an outsider. I was teased a lot for being different, and I never invited the friends I *did* have over because I was embarrassed that our house was a disaster on the inside. We didn't have much money, and my dad was always working to put food on the table, so I was the one who had to clean and maintain things. I became the lady of the house. I went to a parent-teacher conference for Laura, threw her birthday parties, and tried to soften the blow of the divorce for her as best I could. Of course, I was still a child myself, and through all those years, our TV set was my favorite babysitter.

Sometimes, I admit, I was bitter, but I think that emptiness and those challenges propelled me to be ambitious. I remember thinking that if I could somehow get on TV, I could have a better life. I became financially independent at seventeen, started working on TV at eighteen, and bought my own house at twenty-four. Ever since, I've been traveling around the world, telling stories as a correspondent. I *did* create that better life for myself.

But there was a flip side. Since my childhood challenges were driving my achievements, it seemed that the more success I had, the harder it was for me to turn down any opportunity that came my way. I always felt like the next job might not come around. I had a real hustler mentality.

It wasn't until I turned thirty-five that I began to get some perspective on how I was living my life. I had a real body of work behind me now and the confidence to realize that *I* was in control of my career—not the other way around. Recently I was offered the chance to host an Oscars preshow, something I never would have passed up before because it's such a big opportunity. But I don't really like interviewing celebrities on the red carpet; I'm not that good at it, and there are so many other people who are. So I did something that surprised even me: I said no, and I felt totally fine about it.

I'm thirty-seven now. I'm married, I want a child, and I'm trying to maintain this slightly less anxious pace so I can focus on that. But I will always be grateful that I learned early on to run *toward* challenges instead of away from them. And I will always be adamant about the fact that women should be more independent and less reliant on men.

Looking back, I can thank my mom for that lesson. I'm glad my parents divorced and she found her happiness and her independence. I love my parents more than anything in the world. I've worked hard to understand the choices they made, and now that I truly do, I have great relationships with both of them. Making peace with my past was the first step; being grateful for it was the second. Now, at last, I can appreciate the woman those experiences created: me.

---

**LISA LING**, thirty-seven, a former cohost on *The View*, is now the host of *Our America with Lisa Ling* on the Oprah Winfrey Network. She is the cofounder of the Secret Society of Women, a forum for women to anonymously share their secrets.

## 11

What you would and wouldn't do for money or love.

**BY LAUREN CONRAD**

I KNOW I'M NOT THIRTY YET. BUT I WAS EIGHTEEN when I started filming *The Hills*, and I was expected to make very adult decisions, ones I wasn't necessarily prepared to make. My career started supporting the careers of other people—real adults—and, in turn, I felt this big sense of responsibility. Going through all that taught me some important lessons about myself. Plenty of them were about this exact item on the list—what I would and wouldn't do for money or love—so I thought I'd share them with you.

## WHAT I WOULD NEVER DO FOR MONEY:

### 1. Be a phony.

Filming *The Hills*, I grew really close with the crew, and I started to sympathize with them. They're trying to make a good show, and all they need is for you to say this one line or to get this one shot to complete their scene. At first, I didn't think it was a big deal, so I said a lot of dumb things that I thought my producers would want me to say. For example, the editors loved a zinger—a sentence that they could put into a preview for the next show, like "Everything's about to change." But it always sounded so cheesy, and I soon learned to say no when something didn't sound like me. You have to stay true to the kind of person you are.

## 2. Be a manipulator.

One of the biggest fights that I got into with my producer was when I was in Paris. They really wanted me to have this Paris love story, but I had no interest in the boy they chose for me and didn't think it was fair to lead him to believe I did. They kept pushing it—they even told him to try to kiss me. On that episode, he dropped me off at my hotel on his motorcycle, and he kept taking steps closer to me, so I did kind of a backward circle around his motorcycle, then I tossed the helmet to him and ran away. They had to edit around it because I just looked horrified, but I didn't want to lead anyone on.

## 3. Work a job I don't love.

It took me a while to learn this: TV is fun, but it isn't what matters most to me. Now instead of TV shows, I'm focused on writing books, designing my two clothing lines, and working on my lifestyle website. Even though I've managed to make myself very, very busy, I wake up and I'm excited to work. My dad told me that you should always do something you love, because if you do, you never work a day in your life. And now I know he was right.

## WHAT I WOULD NEVER DO FOR LOVE (AT LEAST NEVER AGAIN!):

### 1. Turn away from my family and friends.

I've had relationships that my family and friends disagreed with, and I've made the mistake of choosing the relationship with the boy over them. But I've realized that you should never really *have* to choose. If you have good family and friends, if you are surrounded with people who love you and genuinely want the best for you, there is probably a reason—a good one— why they aren't fans of your guy. If they don't think he's good for you, I would suggest you take a look at your relationship before becoming angry with them. Your family might be right.

### 2. Lie to myself about whether a guy is interested.

When I was in college, I learned that life is not like the movies. I liked this boy a lot—I even helped him move into his apartment. But I couldn't tell how he felt about me. One night after going to a concert with him, I was on the phone with my friend driving home, and my friend said, "I think you need to ask him how he feels," which, of course I hadn't thought of. So I did a U-turn and called him to ask him to come back outside. When he did, I wanted my eighties-movie moment—I blurted out, "I like you. Do you like me?" I waited for him to say, "I like you, too, Lauren," and then cue: a slow-motion kiss, and a song like "Don't You (Forget About Me)." But there was just . . . silence. Basically he liked me only as a friend. I learned not to invest too much in a relationship before I really know how the other person feels.

### 3. Sacrifice my own happiness.

Love isn't always enough. It's a hard lesson because we're raised to believe that it is—it's in every story we hear. But just because you love somebody and they love you back doesn't mean your relationship makes sense or that it's a good one for you both to be in. Having chemistry with someone is important, yes, but the *most* important thing is that the person you're with makes you happy.

## WHAT I WILL ALWAYS DO FOR LOVE, NO MATTER HOW HUMILIATING:

### 1. Care about the small stuff.

I'm not a girl who wants flowers, or doors opened for me. It's the more thoughtful things that really make a difference. During one relationship, I kept trying to poach eggs because I heard it was healthy. I tried for a whole week, but I kept messing up. So my boyfriend at the time bought me a little egg poacher. It was the silliest thing, but it was so sweet. He was letting me know, "I think of you throughout the day."

## 2. One word: karaoke.

I hate it—it's one of the worst dating activities in the world— but yes, I will do it for love. Sometimes embarrassing myself is just *worth* it.

---

**LAUREN CONRAD**, twenty-six, is currently at work on her second trilogy of novels, following her successful L.A. Candy series. She designs two clothing lines, Paper Crown and LC Lauren Conrad for Kohl's, and is the creative force behind laurenconrad.com and thebeautydepartment.com.

That nobody gets away with smoking, drinking, doing drugs, or not flossing for very long.

**BY KATIE CROUCH**

Here's the thing: I've never been one to take drugs or smoke. It's not that I'm a prude. But drugs, depending on the variety, make me either sleepy or dizzy, and cigarette smoke gives me sneezing fits. Also, I have long been privy to the knowledge that twice-a-day flossing is the key to decent breath. Seriously. Have you ever smelled your used dental tape? Flossing equals friends.

Me, I was a hard-core cocktail lady. Nothing froufrou. Take your cosmos and appletinis and give 'em to the amateurs, thank you. In college, I began impressing the boys by ordering what your red-nosed grandfather drank. Martinis, two olives. Manhattans, light on the vermouth. No brandied cherries? Don't bother. Just give me rye, neat, and another one while you're at it.

And what about my literary idols, Maeve Brennan and Dorothy Parker? Those girls were worshipped for their ability to handle a drink and tell a good joke. I'm not saying I followed in their hallowed footsteps. But certainly I tried.

By twenty-three, I had developed the Herculean ability to drink three or four martinis and arrive on time to work the next morning. I was Arthur Frommer's assistant—the real Arthur Frommer, who wrote *Europe on 5 Dollars a Day*, back when $5 bought something more than a battered tampon from a public restroom. He was around 114 years old. I'm fairly sure he'd lost his sense of smell, meaning he missed out on my constant cloud of day-old vodka. But the rest of the office, amused at my youthful tales and impressed at my ability to answer the phones half-drunk, took to handing me vials of Binaca and taking me out for Bloody Mary lunches to get me through the pain.

And the men. Some of the males I happened to find on my alcohol safaris were fantastic. Nice, understanding fellows with good jobs at ad agencies and hometowns in Vermont. But those were extremely rare. Because if you are at the Ding Dong Lounge at 3 a.m. on a Tuesday morning, you will likely be socializing with a less-than-desirable pool of potential mates. I hesitate to write this, as my mother feverishly combs the media for my name, but there were mornings I would open my eyes to find a specimen I would not, sober, have let into my house to change a gasket, much less share my bed. And yet. The twenties! A cheerful cup of coffee, a quick chat about their lives ("Urinal sales? How interesting!"), and I was on with my day.

And then, one night when I was twenty-five, at an after-party at a bar I will never remember, I became unable to stand. This was always my private alarm bell to get a cab home, as even Dorothy Parker never went to bed facedown on a bar floor. I walked out to the sidewalk, and a lurid stranger, seeing my state, began accosting me. He grabbed my arm, pulling me toward an alley. And then, suddenly, a boy who was at my party pushed him away and got in the cab next to me. He was gorgeous. And polite. And wore a gray woolly sweater. I kissed him, and despite my horrible habits and my obvious unworthiness of being with a person like this, we fell in love.

Twenty-five years old in New York and in love. Is there a better place? If so, I haven't found it. We went to museums and concerts. Much time was spent on my slightly wobbly futon. But mostly, we drank. There are so many excellent places to do so in Manhattan. Secret clubs, bistros. He didn't mind because he liked drinking, too. Again, the twenties—they're a whiskey safety zone.

Reader, I wish I could tell you this all ended happily ever after. But I just couldn't rein it in, even for this beautiful man with the woolly sweater, the endless patience, and the shoulders of a Rodin statue. Years passed, and he and I began to have frequent whiskey fights. I became uncertain of my feelings for him, and one night, out with another man at 3 a.m. . . . well.

Needless to say, Rodin Man left me. Would things have

been different if I hadn't been so committed to having a "good time"? Hard to say. The good news (or bad news, depending on how you look at it) about mistakes is that you forget most of them, even big ones. This one, though, I never have.

The next year—twenty-nine—was not good. My patterns were the same, but it wasn't fun anymore. People in Arthur's office were less amused by my hangovers. I had more responsibility at work, which I screwed up. One night after postwork cocktails, I stumbled onto the F train and passed out. When I opened my eyes, I was in Coney Island, the end of the line, and the conductor was calling the police. "No need!" I slurred to him, stumbling to my feet. I was not cute or witty. I was pathetic.

And I had missed my morning plane to my good friend's wedding, where I had promised to give the rehearsal dinner toast. I thought wisdom tooth removal was the worst pain imaginable, but calling a soul sister to tell her I'd traded her rehearsal dinner for a vat of gin tops it hands down. I'd been disappointing myself for a while, but now my friends were getting hurt, too. I had to turn it around. After spending my suitcase's weight in gold on a next-day ticket to my friend's hometown, I made it to the wedding with an hour to spare— and a really great gift to offer.

So, at thirty, I set some rules. Nothing fancy—just basics. For instance: When your crow's-feet begin to creep over your cheekbones, you are too old to be out after midnight more than twice a week. Also: If you love one man, don't flirt and drink with another. It's not rocket science, and yes, it's a less *Sex and the City*–worthy life. But I was able to slow down enough to build my relationships, my career, and a family. And the best part is, I didn't end up old, alone, and living next to the bathroom at *The New Yorker*, which was, eventually, Maeve Brennan's fate.

So enjoy your parties and late nights, friends. Really. *Enjoy* them. But don't be afraid to let them go. Because vice is fun. But waking up hangover-free in a house full of people who love you? That's top-shelf.

**KATIE CROUCH**, thirty-eight, is the author of the novels *Girls in Trucks, Men and Dogs*, and, for girls about half the age of thirty, *The Magnolia League*.

# *What 30 means to me*

## BY BOBBI BROWN

### BEING COMFORTABLE IN MY OWN SKIN

Working in the fashion and beauty industries, I'm often surrounded by young women around the age of thirty who are concerned with things like finding a husband, starting a family, paying their bills, and succeeding in their careers, as well as with how they look. I think the most important thing for them to know is that it's really normal to be freaked out about where you are in life, but those things you want so badly will come in due time. Meanwhile, life will be a lot more joyful if you learn how to be comfortable in your own skin.

This hasn't always come easily for me. I got my start in the industry in my twenties, working as a makeup artist. Growing up around beautiful models meant that I never felt classically pretty. I never thought I was thin enough, and I felt bad about not being blond and blue-eyed. I was also insecure about my height (I'm five feet tall). Now I realize that I was pretty cute, my brunette hair was beautiful, and I looked great. If there is one thing I could do over, I would just have accepted who I was at the time—and maybe hired a tailor to fit my clothes perfectly to my petite frame!

What I would *not* have done is compare myself with models and actresses—and neither should you. I'm fifty-five now, and I've worked really hard to accept that this is who I am. Humor has helped. I collect pictures of myself with ridiculously tall people, from models to basketball players. I don't feel the need to fake that I'm taller—I wear a lot of Converse sneakers—but I do practice yoga, spinning, and weight training. (If you don't lift weights yet, start now, because it gives you incredible confidence, makes you stand up stronger, and all around makes your body look better.) Being thirty is about finding peace with who you are. It's such a great time in life—try to appreciate it. And here's something to remember at every age: Work with the body you've got!

**BOBBI BROWN**, fifty-five, founder and chief creative officer of Bobbi Brown Cosmetics, is the author of six beauty and lifestyle books. She is devoted to philanthropic causes, including Dress for Success.

13

Who you can trust, who you can't, and why you shouldn't take it personally.

**BY LIZ SMITH**

I SOMETIMES CALL MYSELF "THE 2,000-YEAR-OLD gossip columnist" because I've worked in the business for more than fifty years. Along the way, I've had my share of detractors—Frank Sinatra denounced me after I called him a bully in print; Donald Trump tried to buy one newspaper I worked for just so he could fire me; and Sean Penn ran out of a building when we were introduced. But more often than not, I've heard myself described as "too nice" for the gossip biz.

I take that as a compliment. I'm not perfect, but I've never written anything that I knew wasn't true, and I've made a lot of friends in the business as a result. From half a lifetime of lessons learned, here are a few things I've figured out about trust—who deserves it and how to earn it.

## YOU CAN USUALLY TRUST A GAL
## WHO SAYS IT LIKE IT IS.

In the sixties, I was interviewing for a job as an entertainment editor for a glossy fashion magazine. I had met the beautiful and accomplished woman who was stepping down from the position, and one day I called her up and asked her if she would help me set up procedures for the job after I took over. "Why should I do that?" she exclaimed. "I don't want you to do a good job. I want to be remembered as the best." Such candor! She was immune to all my shit-kicking charm, and I admired her for it. Later we became friends, and of course I forgave her everything.

## WHEN IT COMES TO ROMANCE, HEED
## THESE WORDS: TRUST AND VERIFY.

I'm not saying you should be cynical about relationships; it's no fun to go around expecting the worst. But young women are very prone to rushing into love, suspending judgment on guys they're dating. I know I did. I've been married and divorced twice, so I've been guilty of projecting all kinds of romantic qualities onto men whether they had them or not. Follow your heart? Forgive me, but that's the myth of all myths. You should research the man you're with as thoroughly as you'd research which car to buy. What do other people say about him? What's his track record? Be aware of what your situation with him really is instead of what you just hope it will be.

## NEVER TRUST YOUR INSTINCTS WHEN YOU'RE ANGRY.

I can't say I've never acted in anger or in any sense of revenge, but usually my common sense told me when I was about to do something horrible. I also have had a lot of wonderful teachers who kept me from making mistakes. The great Barbara Walters is one of them. She is one of the most ethical people I've ever met, and she came to my rescue more than once when I was about to make a rash decision. Always, always turn to someone wiser than yourself before you act in anger.

## ASSUME YOU CAN'T TRUST ANYONE WHO'S JUST HANDED YOU A CONTRACT.

I've done well for myself over the years, but I would have done better if I'd paid more attention to the fine print on every contract I signed. Get legal advice before you sign anything!

## LIFE'S JUST TOO SHORT TO TAKE EVERY LITTLE BETRAYAL PERSONALLY.

Over the years, I've been attacked by a few people who took offense at things I wrote in my column. And I have attacked back. But down the line, I regretted even bothering. It's a lot of baggage to collect enemies. It's very debilitating and disempowering. So I finally decided it was just better to turn the other cheek.

## THERE ARE NO REAL SECRETS, SO YOU MIGHT AS WELL TELL THE TRUTH ABOUT THINGS.

You don't have to overshare all the gory details, but in the information age, truth telling is the biggest time and energy saver I can think of! I don't have any secrets anymore myself—not since I published a memoir dishing about my marriages and divorces and the rest of it. My philosophy is: Set everything down for the record once and only once. Then move on, make some new stories. What's next?

---

**LIZ SMITH**, eighty-nine, has worked in showbiz and news for more than half a century. She has written gossip columns and celebrity profiles and won an Emmy for her on-air reporting from the battleship *Intrepid* on the fortieth anniversary of World War II. She has raised millions of dollars for AIDS, literacy, and the conservation of New York City landmarks.

**14** Not to apologize for something that isn't your fault.

## BY THE EDITORS OF *GLAMOUR*

CONSIDER THIS AN INTERVENTION. THAT'S RIGHT. We love you and we think you need help. We think you're addicted to "Sorry."

*Glamour* actually conducted a study asking people around the country to keep track of their sorry-saying. And guess what? Women reported that they apologized an average of 5.2 times a day, compared to just 3.6 a day for men.

You use the S-word on your roommate: "Sorry—could I get those jeans back? The new ones you borrowed last month?"

You clear your throat with it at the Monday morning meeting: "Sorry—I have something to add!"

You say it to your server when he screws up your dinner order and you have to send it back: "So sorry, but I ordered the chicken, and I'm actually allergic to shellfish. . . ."

You even utter it when you're waiting for the ladies' room and someone bumps into *you* on her way out. What the *what*? As one woman told us: "I was in line at the ATM, and this guy pushed his way ahead of me. I was irate! But instead of telling him to get back where he belonged, I smiled uncomfortably and mumbled, 'Sorry.'"

Why do we apologize when "sorry" is the last thing we feel? You could argue that as women, it's been drilled into our heads to be sweet, accommodating, and nurturing. But sometimes, "sorry" is a cop-out: It's easier than saying what we think. But there are times when it's *important* to admit that we're annoyed, angry, or maybe just plain fed up. So next time you're about to request forgiveness, ask yourself: "Did I hurt this person's feelings? Inconvenience her? Wrong him in any way?" If the answer is yes, by all means, genuflect away! But if the answer is no, pause and try one of these kind alternatives instead:

*"Hi! You must not have seen me here."* (To the person who just cut the line in front of you.)

*"There seems to be a mix-up, and I'm sorting it out."* (If your boss yells at you for someone else's mistake.)

*"I'm here for you."* (To your distraught friend whose boyfriend caught her cheating, and the truth is, he's the one you're sorry for.)

*"I know this is hard."* (If you've just let your assistant go for being, well, a really bad assistant.)

*"Here's how I can help."* (To your sister, who just asked . . . again . . . to borrow money that you don't have.)

It might feel awkward at first, but keep practicing! And save your mea culpas for when you really mean them. It's the only time they count.

Why they say life begins at 30!

## BY THE EDITORS OF *GLAMOUR*

WHY *DO* THEY SAY LIFE BEGINS AT THIRTY? SOME OF the most accomplished women of our time have shared their theories already in this book. We have one, too.

Thirty is when you stop the comparathon: the rat race that has you constantly looking over your shoulder to see how everyone else is doing at work/love/fitting into their skinny jeans. It's tempting, after all, to see your twenties as your chance to make your mark. So you do your best, and you keep one eye on everyone else doing theirs. It can all leave a girl frantically busy. *Yeah, I kickbox at 6 a.m. with my fittest friends, then do book group at night with my brainy ones! Watch as I keep up with my Pabst-slugging guy pals until 2 a.m.—and then take one home and give him the romp of the century!* Thanks to the comparathon, you approach the end of your twenties accomplished in many things. And exhausted.

Then comes thirty, when federal law all but requires you to reflect. Some friends have gotten married. Others have made partner. Some are starting over from scratch. Some are happy, some aren't, and suddenly, as you process all this change, the comparathon starts seeming . . . kind of lame. Life isn't a contest—beauty, popularity, or otherwise. And there's happiness to go around for *all* of us. Besides, at thirty, most of us start noticing that the most meaningful moments in life so far have happened when we weren't trying so damn hard. Isn't that the way for you, too? A rainy Sunday playing a marathon Scrabble game with your niece. That one amazing kiss with the folksinger from the bar. The compliment from a coworker that, honestly, made you shiver with pride. John Lennon said that life is what happens to you while you're busy making other plans—and in order to savor the magical every-day moments that he was talking about, you have to stop looking around to gauge everyone *else's* progress.

In life, no one else is holding the stopwatch—not those fit friends, not your college classmate who helped found Four-square, not even Oprah. And if you're sitting there holding a clock to your *own* progress, maybe it's time to switch the darn thing off—and then stomp on it. After all, as *Glamour* editor Emma Rosenblum, who recently turned thirty, says: "We're all on different time lines and need to realize that life isn't a race. It's more like one of those huge celebrity walkathons, where everyone's ambling along at her own pace, wearing a really dorky hat and lots of sunblock." By thirty, you should be moving at your own speed. So what if someone else gets promoted first? Or has flatter abs, or more mysteriously perfect hair? Gets pregnant first—or stays gloriously single longer? High-five her. That's *her* race.

Then walk on! And take your niece. She'll be turning thirty someday, and you'll want to tell her how awesome it is. And mean it.

# But Wait!
# There *Is* One More Thing.

BY PAMELA REDMOND SATRAN

Fifteen years older, and theoretically wiser, than I was when I wrote the original list, I find myself still returning to it for guidance with regularity. Hesitating over whether to buy a knockout dress, I'll remind myself that I *do* need something perfect to wear in case the employer of my dreams wants to see me in an hour. What's more, I'll let myself believe that I deserve it. It is my hope that The List will serve you just as well as you approach thirty, and for years to come, too. May you return to it here—in its wonderfully deepened and enriched form—for pep talks, breakup backup, career inspiration, and sometimes just a little reminder that you are not alone in this journey through grown-up womanhood.

But why stop with these thirty things? We're always changing and growing, after all; mightn't The List reach in new directions, too? If you were to add just one more item—to the *Glamour* list as well as your individual one—what would it be? Some very wise women offer *their* suggestions:

## BY 30, YOU SHOULD HAVE . . .

". . . a calm voice, even under pressure. Leave yelling and screaming as a last resort."

—Taylor Swift, singer

". . . the ability to rely on *yourself* for the kind thoughts, encouraging words, and inspiration you need in your life."

—Ann Curry, coanchor, the *Today* show

". . . a job that makes you happy every day."

—Portia de Rossi, actress

". . . a sense of humor, especially when it comes to yourself."

—Lea Michele, actress and singer, *Glee*

". . . enough courage to say your feelings out loud."

—Kim Bonnell, my Glamour List partner

". . . a sharp tongue, and the restraint to use it wisely."

—Lisa Leslie, former pro basketball player

". . . a European adventure with an adorable guy—whom you don't end up marrying."

—Joy Behar, comedian, cohost of *The View*
and host of *The Joy Behar Show*

". . . a signature drink—even if it's a Shirley Temple."

—Susan Cernek, fashion development director,
*Glamour*

## BY 30, YOU SHOULD KNOW . . .

". . . that it's okay to let guys open the door and pay for your tuna melt."

—Kathy Griffin, comedian and star of
*Kathy Griffin: My Life on the D-List*

". . . how to treat yourself so that your employers and romantic partners and friends and even your children know how you want to be treated."

—Kimora Lee Simmons, designer, executive producer, TV
personality, and fashion editor of the Style Network

". . . that revenge is sweet, but sometimes simply moving on with your fabulous life and forgetting all about what's-his-name is even sweeter."

—Meg Cabot, author, *The Princess Diaries*

". . . that having great girlfriends is better than having a bad boyfriend."

—Lisa Ling, former cohost of *The View* and now host of *Our America with Lisa Ling*

". . . how to make a grand entrance and a graceful exit."

—Patricia Chao, music critic and author of *Mambo Peligroso*

". . . how to leave people happier than when you found them."

—Rachel Roy, designer

". . . that even though not everything gets better after thirty, you'll be happier and more confident—so you won't really care!"

—Georgina Chapman, designer

My own idea for the thirty-first item? That you should seek inspiration every day, and hopefully, this book has offered you some. Because every woman needs to stop sometimes at the great railway station of life—on the evening of her big birthday, or the end of a big love affair, or even an ordinary afternoon—and take stock of where she is, how she got there, where she's going, and why.

That's what you're doing right this very minute. You've already started. And you're already there.

# To Send You
# on Your Way . . .

**B**y now you know that Maya Angelou did not, in fact, write the original "30 Things" list. But do you know what she *has* done, right here, just for you? Written one of her very own—full, incidentally, of things for a woman's home, kitchen, and bookshelf. "A woman needs to surround herself with objects that speak of her own worth," Dr. Angelou explains. Too often, she believes, we don't—but these precious possessions remind you that you deserve the best. "I hope a woman buys these objects inexpensively," Dr. Angelou notes, "and knows that their true value, like hers, is more than meets the eye." Every one of us will have our *own* list of thirty treasures for the home. This is Maya Angelou's.

# *My 30 Things*

## BY MAYA ANGELOU

1. A book stand, and on it:

2. A good dictionary

3. A *Roget's Thesaurus*

4. *Sula* by Toni Morrison

5. *The Color Purple* by Alice Walker

6. Poetry by Edna St. Vincent Millay

7. *A Room of One's Own* by Virginia Woolf

8. *The Heart of a Woman* by Maya Angelou

9. *The Selected Poems of Nikki Giovanni*

10. *Atlas Shrugged* by Ayn Rand

11. *The Kitchen God's Wife* by Amy Tan

12. *The Woman Warrior: Memories of a Girlhood Among Ghosts* by Maxine Hong Kingston

13. *The House of the Spirits* by Isabel Allende

14. A silver punch bowl and matching cups

15. A silver coffee serving set and a silver tea serving set

16. With all this silver, you should always have silver polish on hand. When a silver set is polished and shining, it tells a woman that she is worthy of the best because she *is* the best.

17. Four beautiful secondhand matching cup and saucer sets

18. A few beautiful secondhand glasses—
    they don't have to match.

19. A popcorn popper

20. A beautiful bowl

21. A comfortable robe in which to lounge

22. An elegant robe to wear when one has company staying over

23. A well-fitting, tailored suit

24. A beautiful dress to knock folks' socks off

25. A good cashmere sweater

26. *Another* good cashmere sweater

27. A pair of slacks

28. A pair of jeans

29. A pair of running shoes

30. And a good pair of dress-up shoes. They should be really
    wonderful, even if your skirt is long and nobody else can
    see them.

---

**MAYA ANGELOU**, eighty-four, is hailed as one of the greatest voices of contemporary literature. She is an author, poet, and speaker. She has written thirty-one books, ten of them national bestsellers, including *I Know Why the Caged Bird Sings*. Dr. Angelou has also received over fifty honorary degrees, served on two presidential committees, and has been awarded both the Presidential Medal of Arts and the Lincoln Medal. She currently serves as a lifetime Reynolds Professor of American Studies at Wake Forest University.

# Acknowledgments

We have a confession: We made this book for a very selfish reason. We made it because, like all women between the ages of, oh, twelve and one hundred, we were dying to get our hands on an Adulthood Instruction Manual. (Yes, even *Glamour* editors feel clueless sometimes.) And you know what? We're happy to say we feel quite a bit more sure of our footing with this book in our handbag, and there are a lot of women to thank for that.

First, there's *Glamour* columnist Pamela Redmond Satran, without whom it wouldn't exist at all. She wrote the original list, nurtured it as it blossomed into a worldwide phenomenon, and encouraged it to grow even further in these pages. And there's Judy Coyne, the former *Glamour* executive editor who helped polish The List's very first drafts and publish it in the magazine.

We would also like to thank *Glamour* executive editor Lauren Smith Brody, who helped shape this book in its early stages, and *Glamour* editorial development director Susan Goodall, who oversaw the project from start to finish. Then there's *Glamour* contributing editor Genevieve Field, who edited the thirty-one essays, and *Glamour* associate editor Jessica Duncan, who brought all the pieces together and kept the book in motion. None of this could have happened without the help of *Glamour* editors Marina Khidekel, Emma Rosenblum, Margarita Bertsos, and Baze Mpinja.

*Glamour* would also like to thank: Alison Ward Frank, Geraldine Sealey, Lauren Iannotti, Andrew Young, Sheila Maldonado, Talley Sue Hohlfeld, Tommy Dunne, and Damian Fallon. We're thankful for the enthusiasm of our partners at Hyperion, namely president and publisher Ellen Archer; editor-in-chief Elisabeth Dyssegaard; senior editor Christine Pride, who worked closely and passionately to make the book better; and her helpful assistant Kiki Koroshetz.

We are especially grateful for our wonderful contributors, who opened their hearts to us and shared their stories. But most of all, credit goes to the thousands of women who found that original "30 Things" list and made it their own. Thank you for sharing.

—*Cindi Leive and the editors of* Glamour